God is Looking for Men

Is He Looking for You?

FAITHFUL LIFE
Publishers

God is Looking For Men; Is He Looking for You?
Copyright © 2019 E. Allen Griffith
ISBN: 978-1-63073-283-7

eBook ISBN: 978-1-63073-284-4

Biblical Family Ministries

P.O. Box 285

Myerstown, PA 17067

Email to eagbfm@comcast.net

(E. Allen Griffith)

Faithful Life Publishers

3335 Galaxy Way

North Fort Myers, FL 33903-1419

www.FaithfulLifePublishers.com • (239) 652.0135

Published in the United States of America

22 21 20 19   1 2 3 4 5

Table of Contents

Preface

Where are the men? Leadership among Christian men is lacking today as never before. There is passion for relationships, sports, business, and many other time consuming activities, but there seems to be little passion for God. Men can be stirred emotionally and physically, but few get excited about the spiritual.

Men were created to be leaders in the home, the church, the workplace, the community and the nation. Men were created to walk with God and serve Him with zeal and intensity. Men are told to invest themselves in things that matter for eternity. But, where are the men who have caught the vision associated with this spiritual adventure? Where are the men who are saturating themselves with the principles and directives of the Word of God? Where are the men who are excited at the thought of seeing a life changed by the power of Jesus Christ? Where are the men who are fervent in prayer, expecting God to do great things in their lives and the lives of others?

There are too many men, young and old, who are content to be saved with the hope of heaven, but satisfied to be dabbling in worldly ways and activities. Rather than sell out to Christ, many want to see how far from God they can stray, but still avoid His judgment. They live on the edge of immorality, and sometimes slip into its clutches. They were perhaps truly born again, but have failed to grow into the man God wants them to be. There is always an excuse, always someone or something to blame, but never a reason sufficient for God.

It is hoped this book will find its way into the hands and hearts of men who want more out of their walk with God than what they experience now. Many men have ignored their spiritual potential instead of looking for and claiming all that is available to them in Christ.

This text is written to challenge every man to step up to the possibilities that await him when he gives his all, to the One who gave all for him. Whether through personal reading, study and contemplation, or in fellowship at a Bible Study or Sunday School class, this book will guide the searching man to fully experience what God wants for him as a man – a man of God.

Introduction

Are you satisfied with your day to day life as a Christian? Is your relationship with God meaningful? In John 10:10, Jesus Christ said, *I am come that they might have life, and that they might have it more abundantly.* Does that describe your life as a Christian? The **life** of John 10:10 is eternal life. We have that, if we are saved. Beyond being saved however, Christ wants us to have **abundant life**. The word translated *abundantly*, in our verse, is elsewhere translated **overmuch, out of measure, exceeding**. I don't think many men are living an abundant, overmuch, out of measure, exceeding life. Is there more to Christianity than most are experiencing? I don't mean the emotional hype that comes with a lot of today's shallow Christianity. I mean a deep and abiding relationship with God that carries us through every trial or trouble. I mean a relationship that gives spiritual perspective to every aspect of life. I mean a relationship that makes every day a spiritual adventure, envisioning what God might do. I mean a relationship where we are expecting Him to do great things in our life, which will bring blessing to us and glory to Him. I mean a relationship where we communicate regularly and faithfully in prayer, with the anticipation that God is going to answer in incredible ways. I mean a relationship where we sense an intimate closeness to God and believe He is personally interested in and involved in our lives.

This book will walk you into the depths of that relationship with God, which begins when we are born again and truly gets sweeter, as the years go by.

In John 6:37, the Lord Jesus said, *Him that cometh to me, I will in no wise cast out.* While that may be a salvation text, it reveals the heart of God for those who seek Him. God spoke to the people of Israel in Jeremiah 29:13 saying, *And ye shall seek me, and find me, when ye shall search for me with all your heart.* In James 4:8 we read, *Draw nigh to God and he will draw night to you.* I don't think you can find any place in Scripture when God turned away people who genuinely sought Him with a tender and broken heart.

How badly do you want the life and experience God wants for you? How much do you want the fellowship with God that lifts Christianity out of mere church going religion into a vibrant walk with your Heavenly Father? **If you really want it – you can have it.**

Chapter 1

Thinking Through the Basics

As we begin this book, I want to ask you to think about some age old questions. They have always stirred my heart. I want to use them to introduce myself to you and I hope you will think about them in regard to your own life. For any man to contemplate; who am I, why am I here, and where am I going, can only stir the heart to evaluate one's individual worth and purpose. I hope you will take time to think through these familiar, but very probing questions.

Who am I?

Here is who I am.

I am a man, created in the image and likeness of God. While I share characteristics with all other men, which distinguish us from angels, animals, women and children, I have unique traits which distinguish me from other men, and make me who I am. I grew up in a particular home setting; so did you. I was the fourth of four children and grew up primarily under the care of a single mom, but she married my step-father when I was a young teen. He was a nice guy when he was not drinking too much, but was never a "father" to me. When I got saved just after graduating from high school (age 18) he threw me out of the house, which made my first year as a Christian, a time of challenge and growth.

I have physical traits of height, weight, eye color, hair color, facial appearance and body structure. I have a modestly high IQ, some athletic ability, but virtually no natural mechanical ability or IT aptitude. I used to play fast pitch softball and tennis. Now I am more suited for ping pong, horseshoes and golf. I am a politically involved Conservative and ran for public office in 2010. I like to sing, but can play no musical instrument. I follow the NFL and some MLB. I really enjoy college football and follow Penn State. I love the NCAA March Madness and root for Villanova.

I accepted Christ as my Savior at age 18 and was called to preach very shortly after being saved. I am a husband, a father of 5, a grandfather of 18, and at this point, a great grandfather of two – and hoping for more. Other than the Lord, nothing means more to me than my wife, my children and my grandchildren and great-grandchildren. There is no one on this earth with whom I would want to trade places. In the midst of all these earthly facts, I am awed by the thought that I have an immortal soul and will live forever in the realm of a new heaven and a new earth, yet to be created.

So, who are you? Think about it, because your experiences have made you who you are today.

No doubt we are very different from each other. Indeed each of us is unique, and much is often made of the things which make us different from others. Some of those differences commend us to other people, while some of them can create scorn or disdain. Everyone has a value system which they apply to other people, and amazingly that can extend even to physical appearance. A person's worth in this world of humanity can be affected by one's height, athletic prowess, academic abilities, wealth or lack thereof. With all the differences that we can identify among us as men however, this truth stands out to me. **The things that matter to God are equally available to all men.**

Why am I here?

In the broadest sense of this question, I realize I am here at God's good pleasure and am called upon in life, to glorify Him in my body and in my spirit. As a Christian, I acknowledge that God has a purpose for my life that can be fulfilled by no other person. In seeking to know and surrender to that purpose, I find meaning for my life, and peace in my inner man. In seeking to fulfill that purpose, I have gone through both good and bad times. I have endured failures, while also rejoicing in successes. I have climbed to mountain tops on some occasions, while falling into the valleys of heartache and confusion at other times. I am challenged to resist temptation, remain faithful, and give myself to my life's work with dedication and fervency. I daily wait on the Lord to lead me step by step, hoping to live in harmony with His desire and plan for my life. In the midst of it all I am to serve the Lord, endeavoring to be the best I can be. I dread the possibility of someday standing before the God who created me, only to find that I wasted my life or even some portion of it, by missing the intent of God for my existence. I tell the Lord often, I am willing for His will. I want to live my life for Him.

So, why are you here? It would be difficult to live a meaningful and satisfying life if we had no idea why we are present on this earth.

Have you ever seriously considered that God has a specific purpose and plan for you? Does that matter to you? If it does matter, have you followed scriptural teaching, which has allowed you to discover that will and plan of God for your life? The Apostle Paul referred to it as: **"...that good and acceptable and perfect will of God".**

3

Where am I going?

Life is a very brief and uncertain experience. While some elements of the scientific community invest many hours and many dollars in the search for ways to extend our existence on this earth, they have failed miserably. 3500 years ago, Moses stated in Psalm 90 that the years of our lives are 3 score and 10 (70), and if by reason of strength they be 4 score, yet is their strength labor and sorrow, for it (their strength) is soon cut off, and we fly away. It is quite amazing that while some countries enjoy an average life span of over 80 years and some only in the low 40s, the world wide average life span is right about 70. In the United States it is about 78. Moses said, when those 70 years or so are passed, "we fly away". Someday, I am going to "fly away". I am grateful that I am a born again Christian, and though I wish I understood more about the spiritual and eternal than I do, I know I am going to heaven. I will leave this life of sorrow, sin, heartache and pain. I endeavor to live this life in light of the life to come. An eternal perspective establishes a safety net for me when I struggle with earthly battles. I live with a twofold and certain hope: **1.** Should I die, I will leave my body behind and enter into the presence of God; **2.** It may be that Jesus Christ, who has promised to come again, will in fact come during my lifetime. If so, I will escape death and be carried directly into heaven. My total being, body, soul and spirit, will be fitted for eternity. Sorrow, pain and death will be no more. So, in simple terms, I am going to heaven. As it says in the 16th verse of the third chapter of the Gospel of John:

> *"For God so loved the world that he gave his only begotten Son, that whosoever believeth in him, should not perish, but have everlasting life."*

So, where are you going? That is really important to have settled.

If you are not sure you are going to heaven, please stop reading here and find the section in the back of this book entitled, ***How to be sure you are going to heaven.***

The three questions we raised are important. Are we just animals along an evolutionary pathway? Is there another mutation coming which will send us on the way to extinction? Did we originate from a single celled something, that suddenly came alive in a mud hole? If so, why are we here? Is there a purpose for man's existence? Is there any purpose for your own personal existence? Is this life mainly about getting as much money, power and satisfaction as possible in 75 years and then being dumped in a hole to rot away to nothing? Are we going anywhere beyond the grave, or is that it?

There are many people who find no real meaning or purpose in life. They try everything imaginable to find some measure of satisfaction. It may be in the collection of all the "toys" money can buy. It may be in the most bizarre and sinful experiences they can imagine. It may be in worldly success. In fact, it may be in religion. When all is said and done, they are left with emptiness.

For a time, the great King Solomon of Israel lived with tremendous frustration. He tried everything human experience could offer – and he had the money to do it. His initial conclusion is well known. In Ecclesiastes 1:2 he wrote, *vanity of vanities, all is vanity.* He went on and said in 1:3-4, *What profit hath a man of all his labor which he taketh under the sun? One generation passeth away, and another generation cometh, but the earth abideth forever.* In other words, the older generations die and new generations come and the world keeps going on, but it is all devoid of meaning.

In time, Solomon developed a totally different view of life and of himself. Meaning was found in reverence for the God who created him. He encouraged young people to walk a pathway of surrender, and to yield themselves to God as early in life as possible. Of course, we are where we are and none of us can change the past. It is what it is, but as long as we have breath, there is a life to live and a meaningful path to follow. We do not have to settle for emptiness. Thank you Solomon. **So, how do we find meaning and purpose?**

Chapter 2

Awaking to God's Challenges

There are many verses in the Bible that cause me to pause and consider their message. They make me wonder where I fit in to their challenge. They are worthy of thoughtful consideration. They were not all written directly to us, but they can apply to us. I hope you will take time to read each one and think about it.

> II Chronicles 16:9: *For the eyes of the LORD run to and fro throughout the whole earth, to show himself strong in the behalf of them, whose heart is perfect toward Him.*

In this passage of scripture a prophet named Hanani came to Asa, the king of Judah and rebuked him. Asa had established an alliance with the heathen king of Syria in order to defeat Baasha, the king of Israel. Hanani accused Asa of having, "relied on the king of Syria, and not relied on the LORD thy God." Then Hanani told Asa of the willingness and desire of God to find someone whose heart was perfect toward Him, so He might show himself strong on behalf of that devoted believer. **I think He is still looking.** Is He looking for you? I am sure He is.

> Ezekiel 22:30: *And I sought for a man among them, that should make up the hedge and stand in the gap before me for the land, that I should not destroy it; but I found none.*

In this text we find the Lord rehearsing the reason He had brought judgment to the nation of Israel. He tells of the failures of His people.

The priests had sinned, the princes had sinned, the prophets had sinned and the people had sinned. Having recounted those sins, He says, I sought for a man among them…but I found none. He was not looking for a "super" man. He was looking for a usable man. He found "none" – **not one**. Does it stir you at all to think that God might want to use you for a special purpose?

> Joshua 24:15: …*choose ye this day whom ye will serve…but as for me and my house, we will serve the Lord."*

Joshua was near the end of his life when he spoke the words quoted above. He was giving a challenge to the people of Israel, as he anticipated his closing days on earth and the end of his opportunity to lead his people. He called on them to make a choice about their life and worship. The question was whether they would fear God and faithfully serve Him in sincerity and truth (see 24:14). Joshua made his choice to serve the LORD and led his family to do the same. Each man needed to make his own choice for himself and his family. **So do we!** I am not sure all men realize the impact they can have on others, especially their own family members. Have you made the choice?

> Isaiah 6:8: …*whom shall I send and who will go for us? Then said I, Here am I; send me.*

Isaiah had just seen a vision of the Lord. He was captivated by God's holiness, which in turn convicted him of his own sinfulness. Through the cleansing power of God he was forgiven of his sin. In response to the call of the Lord, "Whom shall I send, and who will go for us?" Isaiah volunteered with those now celebrated words, "Here am I, send me." **Have you ever said that?** I have become convinced, not enough men have made the offer.

I Samuel 17:29: *Is there not a cause?*

David was but a young teen. He was at the beginning of life, when he visited the battle front of the war between Israel and the Philistines. He witnessed the mocking of the LORD and the LORD'S people by the giant Goliath. He could not walk away. He felt compelled to uphold the cause of God by standing alone in a battle he could not humanly expect to win. He surrendered the best of his talents and skills to the hand of God and went forward. He stood for a cause that was greater than himself, and a cause that was worthy of his total devotion. **What cause motivates you?**

Acts 9:6: *Lord, what wilt thou have me to do?*

This verse is quoting the Apostle Paul just after he trusted Christ as his Savior. He asked a simple question that seems like a logical response to God from anyone who has just received forgiveness of their sins and the gift of eternal life. We could wish every new believer would demonstrate such openness to the desire of God. How many ask, Lord what wilt thou have me to do? **Did you ever ask?** I doubt that God would respond by saying, "I don't care what you do." He had something for Saul (Paul); I think he has something for you.

Exodus 32:26: *Who is on the Lord's side? Let him come unto me."*

These are the words of Moses. They were given as a challenge to the people of Israel since many of them had participated in idolatrous practices. Only the sons of Levi responded to the call for spiritual faithfulness, and rejection of wicked compromise. In this day when churches are weak and wickedness is exploding, one might ask, who is on the Lord's side? **Are you?** There is no middle ground.

Awaking to God's challenges in these verses and many like them is spiritually intriguing to me. Why? We know each verse was given in a

9

particular historical context and therefore, must be understood in light of the times in which it was given. We need to consider to whom it was given and why it was given, but we should seek to apply each verse to our lives. God is still looking for men to serve Him in unique ways. He is looking for willing servants who acknowledge there is a cause greater than their own. We see the Lord asking men to make a choice about the life they intend to live. We see His challenge for men to reject the ways of the world around them and in fact, to ask God to show them His desire for their lives. We see God's willingness to show himself strong on behalf of such men.

Tragically, at certain times in history God found no such men. Is He still looking for men of godly character and commitment, who will surrender themselves to His call, and yield to His conviction? If he is looking for such men, each one of us should be willing to be the man God wants us to be. **Are you willing?** It does not matter where you have been in life. God will not reject the tender heart of a man who says, "Lord, if you can use me, if you can bless me, I am ready."

Chapter 3

Taking a Big Step

Becoming the man God wants us to be involves spiritual warfare. It will be a many sided conflict and it will not be won quickly or easily. The struggle must be fought however, because there is too much at risk for us to lose the war, or fail to enter into it. It all begins with a **big step.** This step does not win the war; it only begins it. The battles will be innumerable and intense. They will start when we declare to God that we are willing to surrender our lives to Him, and willing for him to change us or do anything with us that He deems fit for His purposes. That declaration is a **big step.** You can express it to Him in prayer. I suggest something as simple as the following:

I surrender my life to you Lord. I am willing for you to change me or do with me anything, that you deem fit for your purposes.

I challenge you to say it. I challenge you to pray it.

It must be emphasized that this step does not win the war; it is only the start of the conflict. For many years I have watched men wrestle with full surrender to the Lord. They know there is a cost involved and they are not sure they want to pay the price. Surrender is tough; follow through is tougher. We will consider follow through later, but let's look at the issues involved with surrender.

In Matthew 16:24-26 we read our Lord's words to His disciples. *If any man will come after me, let him deny himself, and take up his cross* *and follow me. For whosoever will save his life shall lose it: and whosoever will lose his life for my sake, shall find it. For what is a man profited, if he shall gain the whole world, and lose his own soul? Or what shall a man give in exchange for his soul?*

What is at stake in this challenge? We find it expressed as, *saving one's life, losing one's life, losing one's soul, giving in exchange for one's soul.* The proper impact of this text can only be understood if it is pointed out that the terms *life* and *soul* are translated from the same Bible term. "Losing one's life" often suggests the termination of one's earthly existence and "losing one's soul" often suggests one's eternal damnation. In this discussion, the terms life and soul are related to a person fulfilling the purpose of his existence as a human being. Fulfilling that purpose is what gives true meaning to his life. If he misses his purpose, his life is meaningless. Keep this in mind; a man's purpose encompasses both time and eternity. To miss it would be a tragedy of everlasting consequence.

Let's insert those concepts into the text. Only to help us avoid confusion in this text do we enter the dangerous realm of paraphrase. But, here it is. *For whosoever will try to find meaning and purpose for his existence in himself shall lose his true meaning and purpose. Whosoever shall surrender his own search for meaning and purpose in himself for my sake, shall find his true meaning and purpose. What is a man profited if he gain the whole world, but never finds his true meaning and purpose? What would a man give in exchange for finding his true meaning and purpose?*

This passage of Scripture is not in itself a salvation text. It is the challenge of discipleship, but that of course requires that one be saved. There is certainly application to the unsaved. Indeed, what would it profit a man if he gained the whole world and went to hell? Answer: nothing! But Christ was seeking more than one's salvation. He wanted full surrender from those to whom He gave eternal life. Getting saved is but the beginning of life, and that life is going to last forever.

So our Lord puts forth the challenge in this way: *Whosoever will come after me, let him deny himself, and take up his cross, and follow me.* Are you there? Are you willing to be there?

The term "will" means desire. Do you desire to "come after Him"? It means to walk closely behind Him, to be a true disciple. Do you want that? Does it matter to you? Most Christian men seem to be satisfied to be saved, but they don't really want a close and intimate walk with Christ. If we want that walk, there is a threefold requirement laid out in Matthew 16:24.

The first requirement found in this verse is that we deny ourselves. Deny is a strong word which means to have no connection with someone. It was the word used to describe Peter's denial of Christ in Caiaphas' judgment hall. Our Lord said, "Thou shalt deny me thrice". Peter's ultimate words of denial were, "I know not the man." How do we transfer Peter's denial of Christ into the idea of us denying ourselves? Here it is. If someone asked you to describe your goals, hopes, dreams, plans etc. and then said; would you be willing to give up all of those things if you knew God wanted you to go a totally different direction? To say yes would be part one of the **big step** we talked about, and would constitute a denial of self. The simple declaration we suggested above is: **I surrender my life to you Lord. I am willing for you to change me or do with me anything, that you deem fit for your purposes.** The fact is, God may not desire to make any changes in your life at this time. But, will you put everything at His disposal? Will you tell God you are willing to break the connections with your plans for His sake, if he so desires? Will you affirm to Him your desire to find the true purpose and meaning for your life in His will?

The second requirement in the verse for *coming after Him* is to *take up your cross*. The cross of the Lord Jesus was the ultimate fulfillment of the Father's will for Him on earth. It was our Lord's ultimate step

13

of obedience. For us, it is the natural step after denying ourselves. We declare our willingness to surrender our lives to God. Then we take up His will for us. This is not specifically about ministry. He does not want every person on a foreign mission field or standing behind a pulpit, but he does have an intended plan and purpose for each of us. Do you want it? The cross of Christ cost him everything. He even prayed, *If it be possible, let this cup pass from me, nevertheless, not as I will, but as thou wilt.* We do not know where the will of God will take us, but do we want anything less? May we never forget; the suffering of the cross led to the power of the resurrection. The temporal trial led to eternal victory. You will never regret pursuing the will of God. You may be doing exactly what God wants you to do and perhaps you are exactly where God wants you to be right now. Tell Him however, you are willing for change, if that is what He wants. It may take some time to grasp what God may want to accomplish through you, but determine that when you are sure what He wants, you will give everything you have to be successful in your walk with Him.

The third requirement in the verse for *coming after Him* is to *follow Him.* The challenge is more about going in the same way as opposed to following behind. It is the union and likeness of companionship. It is walking the same road. This is certainly not vocational. It is dedication and devotion to the Lord. It is faithfulness and loyalty to His cause. It is spiritual testimony to the privilege of knowing and serving Him. It is refusing sin and resisting the devil.

We are typically locked into the idea of living for God in this life and then going to heaven. Of Course, that is wonderful, because we will be delivered from the sinfulness and destructive ways of our earthly existence. **But what is the meaning and purpose of our lives once we reach heaven?** Of what might Paul be speaking when he says in Ephesians 2:7, "…that in the ages to come he might show the exceeding riches of his grace in his kindness toward us through Christ Jesus."

14

Does one's willingness to, lose his life for "Christ's" sake that he might find it, have only earthly significance, or will it find ultimate fulfillment in the ages to come? I am convinced God's purpose for us will unfold in the ages of the ages to come. I don't completely understand what that will mean, but I know I don't want to miss out on the fullness of God's intent for my temporal and eternal existence. I am certainly not going to throw it away for earthly things. Our Lord exhorted his disciples to lay up for themselves treasures in heaven. In Ephesians 1:18, the Apostle Paul talked about the riches of the glory of his inheritance. Think about his statement in Romans 8:17-18, *And if children, then heirs, heirs of God, and joint-heirs with Christ; if so be that we suffer with him, that we may be also glorified together. For I reckon that the sufferings of this present time are not worthy to be compared with the glory which shall be revealed in us.* Who would be foolish enough to ignore the promise of the eternal for the shallowness of the temporal?

Chapter 4

Paul's Exhortation to Take the Step

Romans 12:1-2 is one of the most significant challenges for a Christian in all the Word of God. The text is well known and often quoted, but its message seems to be ignored by many. Have you ignored it? This exhortation is for every man.

> *I beseech you therefore, brethren, that ye present your bodies a living sacrifice, holy, acceptable unto God, which is your reasonable service. And be not conformed to this world: but be ye transformed by the renewing of your mind, that ye may prove what is that good, and acceptable, and perfect, will of God.*

Let's take the verses apart.

I beseech you therefore, brethren... The first thing that stands out is *brethren*. Whatever Paul has to say is for believers. Every believer needs to understand the message and every believer must respond to the urging. Paul *beseeches* the brethren. The word beseech is a call, an entreaty which seeks response. It is not a command, but it is a strong word, far beyond just asking.

by the mercies of God... Here is the inducement. The persuasion is based on the mercies of God. Paul magnified the mercies of God in the entire book of Romans, but highlights those mercies in chapters 9 -11, just preceding this great challenge in chapter 12. Both Jews and Gentiles were shown to be *vessels of mercy*. Each of us live and breathe by the mercy of God. Jeremiah reminded us in Lamentations 2:22-23, *It is of the LORD's mercies that we are not consumed, because His compassions fail not. They are new every morning, great is thy faithfulness.* Do you sense that in your own life? Where would we be if we got what we deserved?

that ye present your bodies... **Here is the primary challenge of the text.** God wants us to present our bodies to Him. A.T. Robertson says the term "present" is a "technical term for offering a sacrifice". He says the challenge is written in such a way that we are to "do it now and completely". While "body" is usually thought of as distinct from the inner person, it can be used of the whole person. James said the unbridled tongue defiled the "whole body". The body represented the whole person. God wants our whole person presented as a sacrifice, and if we have not done it yet, we need to do it now and we need to do it completely. Paul will tell us more about this, but is there something in the way of you doing this? The song writer caught the meaning when he wrote, "Here's my life, I lay it on the altar". I am amazed that so many men have not done this, but it explains why so many Christian men are struggling in their walk with God.

a living sacrifice... This is not a sacrifice for sin. It is a sacrifice for praise and service. It is a sacrifice that is made to honor God in thanksgiving for our salvation, and to offer ourselves to serve God with our lives. He doesn't want dead sacrifices. He wants our life. Men need to stop playing Christianity and start living it. Stop reading here and go back to **Awaking to God's Challenges.** Reread some of those challenges. If they don't make you think about your life and your relationship to God, what will?

holy... Here is a word somewhat foreign to today's Christian vocabulary. Would you describe yourself as holy? The word always speaks of being separated or different. It means being different for God. There is no need to go into detail or try to specify some list of requirements. It boils down to this simple concept. If someone could hear your words, watch your actions and observe your attitudes, would they recognize in you a love and devotion to God? Why? Why not?

acceptable unto God... To be acceptable to God comes from a term that means "well pleasing", but it conveys the idea of loyalty. Remember David's words, "Is there not a cause?" God wants us to identify with His cause. That is what pleases him.

which is your reasonable service. People act a whole lot more on emotion and impulse than reason. To say an action is reasonable means it is an intelligent response to the circumstances. It has been thought out and considered. God saved us when we deserved hell. He has given us many incredible promises in the Bible. Nothing can separate us from His love. He is preparing a place for us in heaven. In essence He says, "I have given you eternal life; now I want you to surrender your temporal life to me" Don't react. Think about it.

And be not conformed to this world: Here is a command. It is written in such a way that it means to stop what you are doing. To be conformed means to follow a pattern established by someone else. The "someone else" in this case is the world. The "world" in this text refers to the current times in which we live. Things are always changing in the world, and Christians seem to love to jump on the newest band wagon and follow the newest trends. It does not matter what it is. Again, it is not for us to come up with a list of what to do or what not to do. Rather it is our challenge to consider what God says about being a Christian. It is then that we reject those words, activities, actions and attitudes that get in the way of a solid testimony for Christ.

But be ye transformed by the renewing of your mind... Here is another command. Be transformed! This is an amazing word, used of the transfiguration of Christ. Imagine if you saw the Lord Jesus walking the paths of Galilee when he was on earth; would you or anyone, have known he was God in flesh. When he was transfigured, there was an incredible change in him. The glory hidden on the inside was put on display for all to see. Paul uses the same term, *transformed*, to tell us about our life of surrender to God. Anyone who gets saved is dramatically changed on the inside. The problem for too many is that no one would ever know they got saved by what is seen on the outside. Paul says what is on the inside should be put on outward display. However, that change is not a momentary miracle like the transfiguration of Christ. For us, it takes the renewing of our mind. Renew means to make new. We need the renewal, because our minds are a disaster. Our understanding is confused. Our thinking is messed up. We don't make good decisions. We don't see things right. The change we need is very important and it can only happen as we spend time listening to, reading, thinking about and studying the Word of God. **How much have you changed since you got saved?**

that ye may prove what is that good and acceptable and perfect, will of God. Now we come to the purpose of these two verses. It is the search for the will (desire) of God for your life. **DO YOU CARE?** Paul tells us there is a way to prove (test and find out) what is God's will. The desire of God is good for us; it will be pleasing to us, and it will bring completion of purpose for us.

There are a lot of Christian men who demonstrate no more purpose in their lives than unbelievers. Their goals are reduced to vocational success and economic prosperity. Contentment is found in entertainment, sports, politics, etc. Worship and service to God are rooted in convenience rather than conviction.

We are talking about **taking a big step.** Paul's encouragement in Romans 12:1-2 is not to be taken lightly. It was not given to a bunch of missionary appointees. It was for people like us; people who had trusted Christ as their Savior. Once they were saved they needed to figure out what to do next. Think of Paul's own words in Acts 9:6. *Lord, what wilt* *thou have me to do?* In that question was surrender. Paul did not ask for options. He wanted to know what God desired for him. It was not about his next job; it was about his life.

Are you ready to take the big step? If not, why not?

Chapter 5

What is in the Way?

It is only common sense to surrender our life to the Lord, once we have been saved. We are going to exist forever. God has forgiven our sins through the shedding of the blood of Jesus Christ. When this brief life is over we are going to heaven, which is far better than our earthly existence. Then, He is going to create a new earth, where there will never again be pain, sin, sorrow, suffering or death. With those truths and promises in front of us, why would any man refuse to surrender his life to our loving God?

Unfortunately, common sense is not always common. When I talk to men about these things they usually have one or more reasons why they will not yield themselves to the Lord.

In response to the question of why they refuse to do what God asks, they often say, "I don't know". The fact is, they do know. If you have not submitted yourself to God, you do know why. The reason or reasons must be honestly faced. If you don't do what God asks you to do, you will never find real peace and satisfaction in your life. Below is what some men say, or at least convey.

I want to run my own life.

There is an interesting man mentioned in the New Testament. His name was Demas. We do not know much about him, but Paul sums up his Christian testimony in II Timothy 4:19, *For Demas hath forsaken me having loved this present world…* We know from earlier biblical references that Demas had been a friend to Paul and apparently worked with him for a time. Things changed, but we have no idea why. All we know is that he did not want to live for God. He wanted to run his own life. Paul said Demas loved this present world. "World" is the term we saw in Romans 12:2 where Paul said to stop being conformed to this "world". Demas was not just conforming to it, he loved it. The word "love" is not just affection. It means to sacrifice yourself for something. We are supposed to "love" God. Demas was saved, as far as we know, but he wanted to do his own thing. I think of Paul's words to the believers in Corinth. In chapter 6:19-20 of his first letter to them, he said, *…ye are not your own, for ye are bought with a price…* What could possibly make us think we have the right to run our own life? Take some time to think about this matter. This is serious business.

I am afraid.

Fear is common among us. We can be afraid to present our bodies as a living sacrifice, because we don't know what changes God might want to make in us. If we knew what God wanted, we might be more willing to surrender. Then again, we might not. God does not make bargains. He makes promises. He will never give us more than we can bear. He will never leave us nor forsake us. But he does not bargain. Proverbs 3:5-6 conquers fear when the text says, *Trust in the LORD with all thine heart; and lean not unto thine own understanding. In all thy ways acknowledge him, and he shall direct thy paths.*

Of course, sometimes men are afraid to surrender, because they know exactly what changes God wants to make in their lives. Jonah was unique in many ways, but he is a good illustration of our point. He knew what God wanted him to do, but he wanted no part of it. He did not cry out in surrender until he was in the whale's belly. Be careful! It is no fun to be in the belly of a whale.

I can't trust God.

There are a lot of men who have been hurt in life, and they basically blame God. They think life has been unfair to them, and while God could have changed things to help them or protect them, He didn't. Cain failed to see the importance of a blood sacrifice. When his offering to God was refused, he got angry with God and hated his brother. He killed Abel and then in rebellion, became a fugitive and a vagabond. He no doubt thought God could have graciously accepted his offering, but would not. Of course, Cain could have accepted God's invitation to bring a proper offering, but instead he blamed God for his woes.

On the other hand, I marvel at young men like Joseph and Daniel who had terrible experiences in their teen years. Joseph was sold into slavery by his own brothers. Daniel was taken into captivity by the military forces of Nebuchadnezzar. Both of them could have blamed God and turned from Him. Instead, they both yielded to God and were blessed for the rest of their lives.

Are there issues in the way of your full submission to God? Has something undermined your trust in Him? If so, the devil has you right where he wants you. Why? Because you have found a way to justify your resistance to God. Actually, if we can learn the lessons God wants to teach us through the hard times we have experienced, we can be stronger men than most. **What are you going to do?**

It will cost me too much.

Three of the Gospels tell of a young ruler who came to talk to the Lord Jesus about what he had to do to inherit (receive or possess) eternal life. He affirmed his testimony of following the commandments. Of course, his **doing** could never secure eternal life. The Lord Jesus put him in a position that exposed his personal idolatry. The Lord challenged him to sell all he had, give the proceeds to the poor, and then come and follow Christ. When he considered the challenge, it defeated him, because he was very rich. The Lord did not want the young man's money. He wanted his heart. Wealth did not keep the young man from getting saved, but his wealth was what he worshipped. He wanted salvation, but no part of surrender. God has saved, blessed and used many wealthy people. They saw their wealth as His gift to be used for His glory. Some people make wealth their god.

I doubt that the wealth of Peter, James and John approached the riches of the young ruler, but Christ challenged them to follow him too. Their testimony in Luke 5:11 is, *they forsook all, and followed him.*

Thankfully, there is nothing we can do or must do in order to be saved. We face the reality of our sin, we reject our sinfulness, and put our faith in the substitutionary death of Christ. Eternal life is a gift from God. We cannot earn it and will never deserve it.

Once we are saved, God makes no apology for demanding our life be devoted to Him. What would it cost you to fully follow Christ? Is the price seemingly too great to pay? God does not want your dollars, He wants you! **What might it cost you – not to surrender?**

It's too tough to stand alone.

There is no doubt that complete surrender to the Lord will leave many men standing alone. From my perspective, that is what makes a man. It is when we look around and find no one else to support us in doing right, that we are driven to the Lord. Paul wrote in II Timothy 4:15-16, *At my first answer no man stood with me, but all men forsook me...notwithstanding the Lord stood with me and strengthened me...* Sometimes it is hard to know what is right, but when we know what is right, we must do it. I remember hearing the story of two Christian men who worked at the same business. The one was harassed often for being a believer and living for Christ. When the other man was asked why he never suffered, his answer was, "Nobody here has found out that I am a Christian." I marvel at unbelievers who are willing to stand up for their views, and they don't care whether anyone agrees with them or not. Christians are supposed to be ambassadors for Christ. We are more like the secret service. Daniel stood alone. Stephen stood alone. Paul stood alone. If necessary, **will you stand alone for Christ?**

I have gone too far into sin.

There are any number of men who think they have totally lost their testimony for Christ and therefore are somehow unworthy and unusable. The fact is, we cannot change the past. God is gracious and merciful. He is willing to use the man who repents of sin and failure, in favor of surrender. One of the greatest stories in the Old Testament is the conversion of Manasseh, found in II Kings 21 and II Chronicles 33. This wicked king led Judah into sin which was worse than the heathen. Under God's judgment Manasseh humbled himself and repented of his sin. His son Amon followed him to the throne and committed the same sins as his father. While Manasseh lost his son, it appears he was able to impact his grandson Josiah. Josiah followed his father Amon to the throne, but led Judah in one of the great revivals of biblical history. No man, even a Manasseh, has gone so far into sin that God will reject his broken heart. King David's testimony in Psalm 51:17 offers hope to every man. He wrote, *The sacrifices of God are a broken spirit: a broken and a contrite heart, O God, thou wilt not despise.* As long as God leaves us here we can be used for His glory. **No matter where life has taken you – present your body, a living sacrifice to God. Do it now. Do it completely.**

So, if something is in the way of your total surrender to God, what is it? I have suggested some of the things I have heard and witnessed, but each one of us has our own story. Too often men complain that if others had been through what they had been through, they would not surrender either. Hopefully you are reading this and are able to testify that, in fact, you have presented your body as a living sacrifice to God. If you have yet to do it, now is the time. In I Corinthians 10:13, Paul reminds us that the testing experiences of life are common to man. None of us have suffered things that others have not already faced. His point was that people have gone through difficulties of all kinds and come through them with a close walk with God. That means we can too. **This is a matter of choice. I challenge you to get down on your knees. Tell God you are taking your hands off the controls of your life and you are surrendering everything to Him. Don't just think about it. DO IT!**

Chapter 6

Identify Weaknesses and Vulnerabilities

The step of presenting our body as a living sacrifice to God is extremely important in our Christian walk. It can be a battle to finally get to that point. Most men think that such a huge step brings victory to our lives. The truth is, as we said earlier, yielding to the Lord in full surrender does not win the war; it only starts the war. The devil does not want men saved, but once they are, there is nothing he can do to get them back. His goal at that point is to neutralize them through spiritual defeat. When a man gets serious about his walk with Christ, he gets the devil's attention. Once we surrender our lives to Christ we need to face the reality of the conflict to come, and prepare to win it.

I remember being stirred by a Bible teacher when he said, "Whenever you take a step for Christ get ready to be tested." That warning has proven to be helpful over and over again. Thankfully that same teacher introduced Christ's words from Matthew 26:41. He said, *Watch and pray that ye enter not into temptation: the spirit indeed is willing, but the flesh is weak.*

Who wants to fall into temptation? No one who has a heart for God. Men want to live in victory – *the spirit is willing.* As we all know however, *the flesh is weak.* The flesh can be understood as our proneness to sin, which takes over when we are living in our own strength. So what do we do? The warning from Christ was to *watch and pray. Watch* means to keep alert and stay awake. *Pray* means to beg God for help.

No saved man starts his day hoping to find a sinful opportunity. At the end of the day however, many men have entered into temptation. They never saw it coming. They were not alert and their weaknesses were exposed. Believe me, I know from my own experience.

Getting frustrated with people can be a problem. It can be what they say or how they say it. They tell the joke or the lie. They spread the rumor. They treat people unkindly. On it goes, but – what does it do to you? Sometimes people have to be confronted, but the challenge in our discussion is whether or not, in dealing with the person, you are tempted to sin. Be alert, prepare yourself spiritually, so you don't **enter into** the temptation. Avoid those people. Walk away. Begin to seriously pray for them, but don't stumble over people and be taken down by sin. In Ephesians 4:26, Paul said, *Be ye angry and sin not.* That challenge can be like walking a tight-rope.

Maybe you have a temper problem. You know, in certain situations you tend to give way to anger. You may apologize later, but you have to get beyond those kinds of experiences. It must stop! What are you going to do? The Savior tells us the flesh is weak and we know it. Get hold of a Bible text and memorize it. Maybe Proverbs 14:17 would help. *He that is soon angry dealeth foolishly: and a man of wicked devices is hated.* How about verse 29 of the same chapter. *He that is slow to wrath is of great understanding: but he that is hasty of spirit exalteth folly.* Think about your life and testimony. Are you known as a guy with a temper? Is that what you want? Temper cost Moses the Promised Land. It has cost many men the respect of friends and loved ones.

Perhaps your battle is with sensual things or disgusting habits. You have been defeated too many times, but you know you have to get this conquered. We have already emphasized, *the flesh is weak* – and the flesh is not going to get any stronger in fighting off temptation. That is why Paul wrote in Romans 13:14, *Put ye on the Lord Jesus Christ and make not provision for the flesh to fulfill the lusts thereof.* That is a great text for us. To put on Christ is to avail ourselves of every provision He has made for us to live the Christian life. We will get to some of that later. For now focus on this: *make not provision for the flesh to fulfill the lusts thereof.* I had a great friend who is now with the Lord. For years he battle with smoking. He knew it was hurting his testimony. From time to time he would be tempted and would pull his pack out of his pocket. Then he would often say, "I hate these cancer sticks." I would taunt him and say, "Who bought them and gave them to you?" Of course, he bought them. He walked in the store, he picked them up, he paid for them, he carried them around in his pocket. **He made provision for the flesh to fulfill its lusts.** If he did not have them in his pocket all the time, he would have had a chance at victory. We know our weaknesses. We would be foolish to continue to put ourselves in settings where we are likely to fall. You probably know what that means in your life.

Anything sensual can be a terrible taskmaster. We need to guard where we go and what we see. The lust of the eyes has taken down too many men. No one can handle the sensual, but men make provision for it. The TV, telephone, computer, and the wrong places will destroy our lives. We would be fools to think we can get away with dabbling in that kind of sin. In Job 31:1, Job said he had made a covenant with his eyes to keep himself from thinking about a maid. In Psalm 101:3, David said, *I will set no wicked thing before mine eyes.* Our opportunities to see and dwell on sensual things is multiplied a thousand times beyond what those men experienced. Will we win the war or will Satan walk right over us?

One of the toughest battles to win is when **there has been some type of addiction or stupefying practice like the use of alcohol or drugs.** I am talking about those things that have a physical hold on us. Addiction has been defined as a mind and body out of control. A man can be on his way to real spiritual triumph in his life, when something goes radically wrong. Friends turn on him, a job is lost, a relationship is broken, a tragedy strikes, and then he plunges into terrible defeat. In times like that, a man will find it very easy to return to some of his worst habits. He just wants to quit on life. All the effort he has made to walk with Christ seems useless. That is not the time to go to the wrong place and be with the wrong people. That is when we must determine to do the opposite of what we feel like doing. We don't want to turn to God at a time like that – **but we must.** We don't want to pray – **but we must.** We don't want to be with spiritually minded people – **but we must.** We want to give in to that sin that has taken us down over and over again – **but we must not.** In times like that, we don't feel like God is near us at all, but we must claim God's promise in Hebrews 13 5b – 6a, *...he hath said, I will never leave thee nor forsake thee, so that we may boldly say, The Lord is my helper.* Don't turn from God. James 4:8 says, *Draw nigh to God and He will draw nigh to you.*

We don't conquer our weaknesses and vulnerabilities in one giant step or one big decision. In fact, though we may conquer some areas, we will always have to face the reality that the flesh is weak. Psalm 37:23 - 24 is a wonderful encouragement for us. It says, *The steps of a good man are ordered by the LORD: and he delighteth in his way. Though he fall, he shall not be utterly cast down: for the LORD upholdeth him with his hand.* Those verses give us a good picture of the believer. Our

30

only goodness is through Christ, but as one of His, there is a way God has ordered for us to live. Along the way, we do fall, but we are not lost, because we are in God's hand and He upholds us. Sometimes we fall hard and can hit bottom, but remember, underneath are those wonderful everlasting arms. We may quit on God, but nothing can separate us from His love.

Growth as a Christian goes like this. We may fall a lot and go down very hard. As we grow, we still fall, but not as often. We may go down, but not as far. We may go down hard, but we don't stay down as long. Gradually we make the climb toward spiritual maturity and success.

Do you have weaknesses and vulnerabilities? Certainly you do. We all do! Gradually, by God's grace, we can completely conquer many of them and get victory over most of them. To do so, we must honestly face them and take necessary steps to avoid falling. Remember the exhortation of I Peter 5:8, *Be sober, be vigilant; because your adversary the devil, as a roaring lion, walketh about seeking whom he may devour.* **Don't let him devour you!**

31

Chapter 7

Do Not Excuse or Justify Your Sin

One thing God will not tolerate is a feeble excuse for doing wrong or refusing to do right. This kind of phony justification is found throughout Scripture. It started with Adam, who when he was confronted by God about eating the fruit of the tree of the knowledge of good and evil, immediately blamed Eve. Who can forget Genesis 3:12, *And the man said, The woman whom thou gavest to be with me, she gave me of the tree, and I did eat.* God did not let him off the hook and we have all been suffering ever since.

Or what about Aaron's excuse for making the golden calf? This is classic. Here is Aaron in Exodus 32:24, *And I said unto them, Whosoever hath any gold, let them break it off. So they gave it me: then I cast it into the fire, and there came out this calf.* I can just see that calf coming out of the fire all by itself.

Then in I Samuel 15, Saul had been instructed by Samuel to destroy all of the Amalekites and everything they possessed. Saul rejected the instruction and decided to save the King and the best of the animals. His excuse was stated in verses 20-21. He said, *I have obeyed the voice of the LORD…and have brought Agag the king…but the people took of the spoil…to sacrifice unto the LORD.* Again, the LORD would have no part of it. In verse 23 Samuel spoke for the LORD and said, *For rebellion is as the sin of witchcraft, and stubbornness is as iniquity and idolatry. Because thou hast rejected the word of the LORD, he hath also rejected thee from being king.* Saul then claimed he did it because he was afraid of the people. There is no end to the excuses men will use for not obeying God's Word, but sin cannot be justified

Do you have excuses?

Excuse making began with blaming somebody else. Today it is probably the most common way men justify their sinfulness. The simple fact is: people will fail us, so we have to get our eyes off people. We must accept responsibility for ourselves. A good commitment to make for our own spiritual well-being is this: **I will blame no one else for what I do wrong.**

Another common excuse is, **I am sick of the hypocrites**. This is typically used to justify unfaithfulness in worshipping at church or serving Christ in other ways. The term hypocrite actually means actor. It is someone who pretends to be someone else. There are many pretenders in Christianity. If they are our excuse for doing wrong, are we any better than they? Ignore them. Do what is right.

Others protest; **why should I care, others don't?** If we measure our Christian life by what other men do or don't do, we are in trouble. II Corinthians 10:12 helps put things in perspective. Paul wrote, *For we dare not make ourselves of the number, or compare ourselves with some that commend themselves: but they measuring themselves by themselves, and comparing themselves among themselves, are not wise.* A man needs to figure out who he is and who he wants to be. It does not matter what other men do and if we compare ourselves to them, we can only lose the spiritual battle.

That is just the way I am is a pretty common, but miserable excuse for sinful living. Actually, it is quite a confession of spiritual apathy and complacency. When God gives us life He expects growth and change. Our Lord was not happy when he ordered John to write the letter to the Laodiceans in Revelation 3:15-16. He said, *I know thy works, that thou are neither cold nor hot: I would thou wert cold or hot. So then because thou are neither cold nor hot, I will spue thee out of my mouth.* I read that to mean – You make me sick! It is a sad commentary on any Christian who is satisfied with spiritual mediocrity. May the Lord help us break the pattern of besetting sins in our lives.

I had a bad home life growing up. Some men had it worse than others when they grew up, but nobody had it perfect. I never want to diminish what you may have faced as a young person, but here is the thing. If how we grew up is a legitimate excuse for a sinful life, how can there ever be hope for the generations to come. How can bad family patterns ever be broken? There are things about my early life that could defeat me if I dwelled on them. I know however, we cannot change the past. We have to let it stay in the past, so we can move on to be what God wants us to be. Being failed or hurt in our early years can provide motivation for being better. It cannot serve as a pretext for the lack of spiritual growth or genuine commitment to Christ.

I have tried, it doesn't work. When a man uses this excuse it reveals that his effort to surrender was tagged to certain expectations. It is not unusual for someone to imagine that if he does good things, then God should bless him in special ways. When expectations are not fulfilled, some quit on God. Peter was on dangerous ground when he said to the Lord Jesus in Matthew 19:27, *we have forsaken all and followed thee; what shall we have therefore?* The Lord told him of eternal blessings, but Peter faced real challenges in his earthly walk. We need to surrender to God, because He is God, not because of what we hope to get out of it.

Proverbs 28:13 says, *He that covereth his sins shall not prosper: but whoso confesseth and forsaketh them shall have mercy.* God wants us to confess our sin and then stop doing it. One of the reasons we continue to be defeated by sin is an underlying sinful attitude. Something might be sinful, but it is okay for me because I have an excuse. Romans 12:9 tells us to *Abhor that which is evil and cleave to that which is good.* In Psalm 97:10 we are told, *Ye that love the LORD, hate evil.* I have found it easy to hate evil, but I have learned I must come to the place where I hate the sin and evil **in me.**

It is time to move forward toward real success and victory in our walk with Christ. Remember Psalm 37:23-24. David encourages us by telling us the steps of a good man are directed and established by the LORD. God delights in his way. Even if we stumble in our life, we will not be completely destroyed, because the LORD holds us with his hand. Did you ever fall? Me too. God will help us and hold us up as we genuinely seek fellowship with Him. If you want a joyful, satisfying, meaningful life, it is available.

Chapter 8

Understanding our Relationship with God

It is common to tell people that Christianity is not a religion; it is a relationship. That is great truth, but do we understand it and do we enjoy all that is available to us as children of God. Understanding our relationship with Him is foundational to desiring and experiencing fellowship with Him.

Different biblical terms describe the various aspects of our salvation. Consider some of them. We are **saved**. That is a precious term. It refers to the fact that as sinful men we deserve to go to Hell. Being a Christian means we are "saved" from going to hell. We are **redeemed**. Redeem means to purchase. On the cross Christ paid the price for our sin. Paul wrote, *ye are bought with a price*. We are **justified**. Justification was a legal term in Paul's day. It meant to be declared righteous by a judge. We are guilty, but because of Christ, God declares us to be righteous, in the court of heaven. We are **forgiven**. That means our slate of sin has been wiped clean by God. We are **reconciled.** Before we were Christians, we were enemies of God and separated from Him. We find peace and reconciliation with God through the shed blood of Christ. So goes the wonderful list of terms that describe what we enjoy as believers. There is another term which deserves our attention. It is the best term to describe our relationship with God. The term is, **born again**.

To be born again means we have been spiritually born into God's family. The biblical term **regeneration** describes this work of God wherein He gives us eternal life and we become His children. John 1:12-13 says, *But as many as received him (Christ), to them gave he power to become the sons of God, even to them that believe on his name: which were* **born**, *not of blood, nor of the will of the flesh, nor of the will of man, but* **of God**. That changes everything. Each of us, who has been born again, has God as our heavenly Father. This makes our salvation very personal. It opens the door to true fellowship with the God who created us.

The first truth that strikes me about being born again, is how often the Lord Jesus talked to his disciples and used the terms, *your heavenly Father* and *your Father, which is in heaven.* The Old Testament believer could never personally call God his Father. He was LORD, God, Lord GOD, but never Father. In this age, we can call Him Father. I confess that growing up without a father may have kept me from fully appreciating this new relationship for some time. Fatherhood was very impersonal to me. I believe getting a father-in-law who loved the Lord, and then becoming a father myself, helped a lot. Then I learned that God said He was a father to the fatherless. It all started to take on great meaning. Now it is very personal for me, and I hope it is for you. We have a Father in heaven.

As we read the Scriptures we learn much about God as God, but we also learn more about God as our Father. We learn of His personal interest and involvement in our lives. In Matthew 10:29-31 the Lord Jesus said, *Are not two sparrows sold for a farthing? And one of them shall not fall on the ground without* **your Father**. *But the very hairs of your head are all numbered. Fear ye not therefore, ye are of more value than many sparrows.* God is personally interested in each of us. It matters to Him what happens to us, and what challenges we face. The very hairs of our head being numbered, is God's way of telling us He knows about every detail of our lives. He is aware of every difficulty, and attentive to every need.

We learn from Scripture that God loves each of us personally and wants us to seek him personally. In John 16:26-27 our Lord said, *At that day ye shall ask in my name: and I say not unto you, that I will pray the Father for you: For **the Father Himself loveth you**, because ye have loved me, and have believed that I came out from God.*

It would be easy to assume that since Christ had been on the earth and is now in heaven, we should ask him to ask the Father for the things we desire. The Lord Jesus said, He was not going to pray to the Father for us. The Father wants us to personally come to Him. The reason is that He Himself loves us. We approach God's throne in Jesus' name, but we are invited to speak directly to our heavenly Father. We need to think about what we are doing when we bow our heads in prayer. We need to envision ourselves stepping into God's throne room and having both the invitation and the privilege to talk to Him personally, as our Father. That is not just religion.

Galatians 4:6 and Romans 8:15 help us understand the depth and intimacy of our relationship with God. In these verses we find the term "Abba Father". The first time it is found in Scripture is in the record of the prayer of our Lord Jesus in the Garden of Gethsemane. Mark 14:36 says, *And he said, Abba, Father, all things are possible unto thee; take away this cup from me, nevertheless not what I will, but what thou wilt.*

Abba is an Aramaic word which speaks of the intimate cry of a young child to his father. It is a term reserved for family members, and testifies of closeness and trust. If we think about what was happening in Gethsemane, we can sense the intimate relationship between the heavenly Father and our Lord Jesus.

In Galatians 4:6 and Romans 8:15, Paul applies the term "Abba" to our relationship with God. Without detailing all that is involved in these two texts, let it suffice to say; we will someday receive a glorious inheritance in His presence, as the sons of God. Until that time, we enjoy the childlike experience of speaking to the Father every day in prayer. We approach Him with assurance that, as a loving earthly father is sensitive to his young son in time of need, so our heavenly Father will be responsive to us. This expresses the depth of our relationship with God. We may not feel like we experience what is described in the words Abba Father, but claim it and yearn for it.

In Matthew 6, the Lord Jesus taught his disciples very specifically about the secret life of personal and private fellowship we can have with our heavenly Father. In verse 4, He talked about our kind and merciful acts toward others. The text calls them *alms*. He said we should do them in secret and then our Father, who sees in secret, will reward us openly. In verse 6, He talked about secret prayer. He said, our Father who sees in secret will reward us openly. In verse 18, He talked about fasting. He said we should fast in secret and then our Father who sees in secret will reward us openly. In Psalm 91:1, Moses wrote, *He that dwelleth in the **secret place** of the most High shall abide under the shadow of the Almighty.* If we can grasp the idea of the "secret place", it will put our Christian walk on a level few men ever experience. It is the place where no one else can enter. It is where we meet with God and no one else is aware of it. If offers the quiet experience of meditation, patient waiting, tender tears and intimate prayer. Much of Christianity is public, and that is fine, but our public experience should be a reflection of our secret experience.

John 10:28-29 gives us more incredible truth. Nothing can ever break our relationship with our heavenly Father. I have heard of parents disowning their children. I have been told that at one point when I was very young, my father denied that I was his. That did not change the facts. I was his and he was stuck with the truth. I have heard of parents who took their children out of their will, but that did not change the parent/child relationship. In John 10:28-29, Jesus said, *And I give unto them eternal life; and they shall never perish, neither shall any man pluck them out of my hand. My Father, which gave them me, is greater than all;*

and **no man is able to pluck them out of my Father's hand.** We are secure, not because we are holding on to his hand, but because we are **in** his hand.

Being born again changes everything. We were totally separated from the God that created us. We were not children of God, but in fact were spiritual children of the devil. Now our eternity is secure in Christ. We belong to the Lord, and the door is open for us to actually experience fellowship with Him.

Chapter 9

Experiencing Fellowship with our Heavenly Father

What is Fellowship? The primary term used in the Bible for fellowship is sometimes translated "fellowship" and sometimes translated "communion". The term means to have something in common, to share, or to be in partnership. It is rooted in common experiences and common interests. Paul questioned in 2 Corinthians 6:14, *what communion hath light with darkness?* The answer is obviously none, because they have nothing in common. Maybe we should think about what we have in common with God. Are we interested in the things that are important to Him? Do the things that matter to God matter to us? Could it be that we don't feel a closeness to God, because as we might put it today, we are not on the same page? In James 4:8 James wrote, *Draw nigh to God and He will draw nigh to you.* That is an invitation and promise all rolled into one. Each of us has to decide if we want it. Many don't, and we see the evidence in men who profess to be born again, but have little heart for the things of God. If you don't feel very close to God. Talk to Him. Tell Him you want a close walk with Him; you want to sense a closeness to him and to sense He is close to you. See him as a loving Father, who wants to bring blessing into your life.

Please turn to Hebrews 12 and read verses 5-17. In this passage, we are shown the picture of God being a faithful heavenly Father in the midst of our times of trial. He teaches and trains each of his children how to live in victory over trouble, while developing holiness, righteousness and reverence. If we are going to have fellowship with God, we are going to have to trust Him in every situation. Please follow the verses as you read this brief explanation.

The believers who received this letter were going through a hard time. Their faith was wavering. Verse 5 of our passage quotes Proverbs 3:11 to warn believers to not despise the chastening of the Lord. Chastening is training and discipline. It involves rebuke, which is intended to bring conviction, and it involves scourging, which means discipline. Verses 6-8 tell us chastening is part of faithful fatherhood. Verse 6 begins with, *For whom the Lord loveth he chastens.* That refers to us who are His children. The Lord knows our individual problems and our individual needs. He knows exactly what it will take to make each of us into the man He wants us to be. Verse 9 encourages us to be in "subjection" to him. Subjection speaks of submission and obedience. And we emphasize again that verse 6 tells us, this father/child relationship is based on His love for us. If we can grasp the full meaning of what we experience as the Father's child, we will be awed by His personal care and concern. Instead of submitting and obeying, there is a danger of despising this special work of our heavenly Father in our lives. That is why verse 5 cautions us about "fainting". Fainting is giving up and letting go. If we see a trial as God abandoning us to suffer on our own, we can become very defeated. But, if in that same trial we sense the personal concern of our Heavenly Father for our growth and development, we will bear fruit for His glory and develop great spiritual strength in our Christian walk.

Verse 10 tells us the hard times of life are designed and/or allowed for our profit. They are the pathway to spiritual manhood and holiness – and our Heavenly Father walks with us along that trail. Religion can be very cold and hard. Our fellowship with God is a comforting, encouraging, and learning experience. In verse 11, we are told God knows life can be very hurtful, but those difficult times can produce greater righteousness in our lives, if we learn the lessons God has for us. That is why verses 12 and 13 tell us we should not ever give up, because God will heal us from discouragement and heartache. Nobody wants anymore hurt or trouble. Personally, I have had enough. As a dad however, I know my children had to face some things they did not enjoy when they were growing up. It was only how much I loved them however, that demanded they be trained. They responded because they knew I loved them and now we walk together in sweet fellowship.

Psalm 103:8-14 is another text I suggest you read. There are a lot of hard people in the world who really don't care how we feel or what we have gone through. On the other hand, God has incredible qualities of understanding and compassion. That does not mean He lowers His standards of righteousness when He deals with us, but He takes our weak and failing humanity into consideration as he responds to our struggles with life's battles. How many could wish they had such an earthly father? Look at verses 8-10. *The LORD is merciful, gracious, slow to anger and plenteous in mercy. He will not always chide: neither will he keep his anger forever. He hath not dealt with us after our sins; nor rewarded us according to our iniquities.* Have you come to realize how merciful and longsuffering our Heavenly Father has been toward you? He is faithful and never fails.

Verses 13-14 help us understand why He treats us so kindly and graciously. Think about this picture from verse 13, *Like as a father pitieth his children, so the LORD pitieth them that fear Him.* Pity means to understand and have compassion. Verse 14 goes on, *For he knoweth our frame; he remembereth that we are dust.* As I mentioned, I did not have a father when I grew up, but I saw a bunch of them. Some were pretty harsh. I had friends who were afraid of their father. A father is supposed to "pity" his children. That means he is supposed to understand their struggles, failures, weaknesses and inabilities. Many earthly dads fail

43

their own children. God does not. He understands! I don't want to fail the Lord, but I do. When I fail, I know he will not refuse me when I come back to Him. He wants me to spiritually succeed, because that is when I grow as a Christian.

Keep this in mind however, God is compassionate, but He is nobody's fool. We can't play games with Him. As Paul said in Galatians 6:7, Be not deceived, God is not mocked. However, when God sees we have a heart to live for Him and serve Him, His mercy and grace will be extended to the fullest. These wonderful truths play out in our lives every day. What if God, *dealt with us after our sins* and *rewarded us according to our iniquities*? We would be dead in a day. But, to be born again puts us into a father/child relationship. A good dad sees his children as individuals. He observes their unique qualities and characteristics. While his standards for his home are the same for all, he works one on one with each child. That is what God does with us. Do you sense that? Do you want that?

In 1 John 1:1-10, John acknowledges that our fellowship with God can be broken by sin, but it can be restored through confession. John described the wonderful fellowship he and the other disciples enjoyed with the heavenly Father, through Christ. In verse 3, he informed his readers that they could enjoy that same fellowship and that truly it was with the Father. He warned that if we live in the darkness of sin, that sweet fellowship will be broken. In verse 9, he affirmed that, *if we confess our sin, he (the Father) is faithful and just to forgive us our sin and to cleanse us from all unrighteousness.* This is important! To "confess" literally means to "say the same thing". The Father will forgive our sin, cleanse us and restore our fellowship with Him, if we don't try to whitewash our sin, excuse our sin or deny our sin. If we sin – and we do – He keeps His arms open to us. He invites us to face the truth. As we saw earlier, Proverbs 28:13 makes it very clear. *He that covereth his sins shall not prosper: but whoso confesseth and forsaketh them shall have* *mercy.* Sometimes our shallow Christianity is due to unconfessed and unforsaken sin. If we deal with it honestly, fellowship with our heavenly Father can be immediately restored. In fellowship with Him we enjoy all the blessings that are intended for us as God's children

Chapter 10

Deeper Fellowship Through the Holy Spirit

The moment we are born again we become children of God. It is a work of the Holy Spirit called Regeneration (God giving us spiritual life). Before we are born again, Ephesians 2:1 says, *we were dead in trespasses and sins,* and verse 12 says we, *were without Christ, having no hope and without God.* Being dead in sin means a person has no relationship with God. Though he will exist forever, he will be separated from God for all eternity. Regeneration gives us eternal life and a true relationship with God, as the Holy Spirit unites with our human spirit. The Lord Jesus told Nicodemus in John 3:6, *that which is born of the Spirit is spirit.* In Ephesians 2:19 Paul said, *now we are fellow citizens with the saints and of the household of God* and in verse 22 he said, *we are an habitation of God through the Spirit.* These verses describe our relationship with God, which opens the door to the fellowship discussed in the last chapter. **How do we deepen that fellowship?**

God has provided three specific means of deepening our fellowship with Him, and we must take advantage of them all.

The first is the indwelling presence of the Holy Spirit. Paul wrote in I Corinthians 6:19 that believers are *the temple of the Holy Ghost.* There are two words that can be translated temple in the Bible. The one used here speaks of the inner sanctuary, not just the building. In other words, it speaks of the very dwelling place of God, when He was present in the Old Testament Temple. No one feels it happen, but the moment we put our faith in Jesus Christ as Savior, the Holy Spirit actually enters into us. As He does this, He takes other steps of permanent ministry to us. He places (or baptizes) us into the spiritual body of Christ, which is the Church (I Corinthians 12:12-13; Ephesians 1:22-23). Then He seals us, so we can never be lost (Ephesians 1:13-14). Regenerating, Baptizing and Sealing are all one time permanent works of the Holy Spirit on our behalf, **but what is the purpose of the Holy Spirit indwelling us?**

When I got saved I knew there was an immediate change in my life, but pretty quickly I proved to myself that I was still messed up. Was that true for you? Amazingly, the Apostle Paul experienced the same thing that we go through. As he wrote about it in Romans 7, he drew this conclusion in the 18th verse. He said, *For I know that in me (that is, in my flesh,) dwelleth no good thing: for to will is present with me; but how to perform that which is good I find not.* That verse reminds me of Matthew 26:41. Jesus said, *Watch and pray that ye enter not into temptation: the spirit indeed is willing, but the flesh is weak.* That verse reminds me of Galatians 5:16 which says, *Walk in the Spirit, and ye shall not fulfill the lust of the flesh.*

These verses give a clear picture of the life of a believer, especially a new believer. Even though we are born again and are now on our way to heaven, we still have this problem called the flesh. There is nothing good in it, and though I might want to live right, I am going to keep failing, and giving in to temptation. The only hope God gives me is to *Walk in the Spirit.* If I walk in the Spirit, He will change everything about me. If I don't walk in the Spirit, I can wreck my life, even though I am a believer. There are many men who will testify that they are saved, but their life is a disaster. **This is why the Holy Spirit indwells the born again Christian.**

This is how the Bible sets it up.

Ephesians 5:18 says, *And be not drunk with wine, wherein is excess, but be filled with the Spirit.* I have never been drunk in my life, but I was around a lot of drunkards when I grew up. The alcohol took control of those men. It made them do and say things they would have never done or said if they were sober. In a positive way, Paul is letting us know in Ephesians 5:18 that if we are filled with the Holy Spirit, we will say and do the right things – that we would not do and say, if we were trying to live in our own strength. We don't have to ask the Holy Spirit to fill us. The verse should read, "Allow yourself to be filled". The Holy Spirit is in us. He wants us to experience the fullness of His impact on our lives. **He wants to change us; but will we let Him do it?**

I Thessalonians 5:19 says, *Quench not the Spirit.* To quench means to put out the fire, or it can mean to resist. The Holy Spirit is in us and wants to change our lives. Do we want him to do that? Are we willing to be changed? It is hard for me to imagine a believer not wanting the life changing power of the Holy Spirit working in him, but Paul felt the need to warn Christians not to quench Him.

Ephesians 4:30 gives another warning. Paul wrote, *And grieve not the Holy Spirit...* To grieve means to cause grief or distress. It speaks of the Holy Spirit being brought to the point of disapproving the life we live. In so doing we cut off the normal blessing and guidance we might otherwise receive. The grieving comes from persistent sin in our lives.

Here is how we receive the blessing God intended, when He gave the Holy Spirit to take up residence in us. First, we determine to fully open our life to the working of the Holy Spirit. Further, when we have made wrong choices, we determine to deal with sin in our life as quickly as possible. When we follow these biblical teachings, the Holy Spirit can freely proceed to carry on the work of transformation in our life. The transformation will bring a change in our character. The various aspects of that change are referred to as the fruit of the Spirit. That fruit is identified in Galatians 5:22-23. It is God's method of totally changing us into the man He wants us to be. It will ultimately involve every area of our inner man. **Let's look at it.**

Galatians 5:22-23 says, ***But the fruit of the Spirit is love, joy, peace, longsuffering, gentleness, goodness, faith, meekness, temperance: against such there is no law.*** Let's talk about each trait.

Love: Love is not a feeling; it is an attitude. To develop genuine love involves a total change, by rejecting a high view of ourselves, and replacing it with a higher view of God and other people. It will also involve a change in our view of the world around us. We men tend to be self-centered and look out for our own interests. The initial challenge of love is to put God first in our lives. Then we care for the needs and interests of family and others. At the same time we recognize the danger that comes from loving the world, making sure we are not captivated by its allurements. God wants to deliver us from selfishness and pride, while developing in us a willingness to sacrifice ourselves for the greater cause of Christ. This is #1 on the list of what the Holy Spirit wants to do in deepening our fellowship with God.

Joy: Joy is delight or gladness that has a spiritual basis. It is not related to our circumstances. James said to count it joy when we fall into diverse temptations. That calls for a spiritual perspective that lifts us above the difficult situations we might face at any given time. Joy is an attitude which enables us to look at life from the standpoint of a sure salvation. It is demonstrated in the testimony of the believers, who received the book of Hebrews. In verse 34 of the 10th chapter the writer commended them saying, *(ye) took **joyfully** (with joy) the spoiling of your goods, knowing in yourselves that ye have in heaven a better and enduring substance.* This is an eternal perspective that will deliver us from discouragement, when things don't go according to our plan. We don't need to wallow in defeat or sink into depression. As Nehemiah said to the people of Israel, "...the joy of the LORD is your strength" (Nehemiah 8:10).

Peace: Peace means to "be at one again". The term in this text is not talking about relationships with people. It is peace on the inside. Our life is often filled with turmoil. Sometimes we can fix it, but many times we can't. On the outside things can be in turmoil, but what do those problems do to us on the inside? There are people who are schizophrenic. They have a "divided mind". Peace means to be at one again. God tells us in Philippians 4:7 that we can have a peace that passes understanding, and it will keep or guard our hearts and our minds. If we allow ourselves to be governed spiritually and emotionally by our circumstances, we will live a miserable life. The Spirit of God can give us peace and internal rest, when humanly there is every reason for anxiety. In Isaiah 26:3 we read, "Thou wilt keep him in perfect peace, whose mind is stayed on thee: because he trusteth in thee."

Longsuffering: Longsuffering is attributed to God in 1 Peter 3:20, when He held off judgment of the earth, until Noah completed the ark. It literally means "long tempered". It is self-restraint in the face of aggravation, as opposed to hasty response. It is an attitude displayed toward people more than toward circumstances. It will protect us from foolish actions and allow us time to contemplate a matter, before addressing it. It reflects wisdom, understanding and discretion. Proverbs 14:29 gives us good counsel. "He that is slow to wrath is of great understanding: but he that is hasty of spirit exalteth folly."

Gentleness: "Gentleness" is the translation of a term that might be better rendered **kindness, goodness of heart or graciousness**. It is absent of harshness and intimidation, which we as men often think of as testimonies of our strength and manhood. It is a wonderful quality which is used to describe God Himself in Romans 11:22, where it is translated "goodness" three times. Some will have difficulty harmonizing this term with the next one, but the balance between the two is essential and can only be produced by the Holy Spirit.

Goodness: Goodness is similar to the term above, but it is **moral goodness**, which produces the commitment to stand for that which is right. It has been illustrated with the "goodness" of Christ that caused Him to cleanse the temple. Goodness cannot turn a blind eye to sin or compromise. It was out of that same goodness that our Lord spoke to pronounce judgment on the Scribes and Pharisees in Matthew 23:13-36, where He called them hypocrites, vipers and serpents. Goodness includes a love for truth and righteousness, along with the highest of moral values.

Faith: The context determines that "faith" in this text, may be best rendered passively, as the **faithfulness and trustworthiness,** which are byproducts of genuine belief in God and his Word. Loyalty, allegiance and devotion to the right causes are lacking today. Solomon illustrated the problem well in Proverbs 25:19 when he wrote, *Confidence in an unfaithful man in time of trouble is like a broken tooth, and a foot out of joint.* The pain from each is hard to bear. The writer of the 12th Psalm cried out, *Help, LORD; for the godly man ceaseth; for the faithful fail from among the children of men.* The Spirit of God seeks to produce men of unswerving steadfastness, loyalty and dependability.

Meekness: Meekness, as has been stated many times, is not weakness. The very fact that the Apostle Paul used it to describe our Lord Jesus, tells us, one can be meek while having infinite power and resources readily available to accomplish one's desires or defend one's cause. Meekness has been defined as **strength, power or authority - under control.** It is the restraint of those resources, for the purpose of accomplishing a greater goal. The hymn writer wrote, He could have called ten thousand angels. Christ could have called ten thousand angels, but then the greater cause of Calvary would have been lost. How much spiritual good has been lost, because meekness was foreign to our character. We sometimes only see the immediate and temporal, but determination to gain victories in those areas may blind us to the greater cause of Christ and the values of eternity.

Temperance: Temperance is an amazing term. It means to have power over or control of one's self. It is translated "contain" in I Corinthians 7:9 regarding sensual things and the ability of one to "contain himself". It is translated "temperate" in I Corinthians 9:25 referring to control of one's body, including desires, appetites and actions. The root term of temperance is translated "dominion" in Jude 25 and elsewhere. God has dominion over all things. He has given us the Holy Spirit so we can have dominion over our passions and will.

All of the qualities mentioned above, from Galatians 5, can be produced in our lives, but only by walking (living) in the power of the Holy Spirit. He alone can produce transformation of our character.

Theologian, Lewis Sperry Chafer, in Volume VI of his 8 volume theology, dealt with the believer being filled by the Holy Spirit. He wrote, **Within the range of the believer's experience, there is no indication, manifestation, or identification of either the presence or the activity of the Spirit beyond the noticeable results that He achieves.** That means we are not going to need to jump, spin around, wave our arms, jibber jabber or faint to prove the Holy Spirit is working in us. We surrender to Him. He will gradually, quietly transform our lives.

Think about the man God wants each of us to be and can make us to be, **if we will allow the Spirit of God to have free reign in our lives.**

The man transformed by the Holy Spirit loves God, his family and others, being willing to appropriately sacrifice himself and his desires in the interest of those he loves. He does not love the World, nor does he invest his energies into worldly ways and sinful endeavors. He finds his greatest joy in knowing he is a child of God, and he sees all of life with eternity's values ever before him. While trial and trouble may come his way, his faith is unshaken and he remains faithful to his Lord. Inner peace keeps him emotionally steady and spiritually strong. When faced with provocation, he does not react with sinful ways or words. He considers the matter, and acts with discretion and wisdom. He is gracious and kind, easy to be entreated, and never intimidating or harsh. At the same time, he has strong moral values. He chooses what is right, and will stand alone if necessary. He is dependable. He will be faithful in fulfilling obligations and commitments. He will be loyal to God, and those who love the Lord and His Word. He recognizes God's cause as greater than his own. He will sacrifice his rights in order to achieve the highest spiritual end in any situation. Things don't have to go his way, nor will he demand self-satisfaction, as he seeks the greatest possible good out of every circumstance. He exercises godly discipline in every area of his private and public life, so as to maintain his testimony and stay usable in Christ's service. **This is what God wants to produce in us. Is it what we want God to produce in us?**

Chapter 11

Deeper Fellowship Through the Bible

The first specific means God uses to deepen our fellowship with Him is the work of the indwelling Holy Spirit to produce His fruit in our lives. The second specific means God uses to deepen our fellowship with Him is obedience to the directives and principles of Scripture. Let's begin this chapter with a few important concepts:

First, it has been well said that 90% of the will of God is found in the Word of God.

Second, the Holy Spirit will NEVER lead us contrary to the teachings of the Bible.

Third, if we have trouble comprehending parts of the Bible, or struggle with seeming contradictions; the problem is with our knowledge and understanding of God's written Word.

In 2 Peter 3:16 we are told there are things in the Bible that "are hard to be understood". In 1 Peter 1:11-12, Peter said even the prophets struggled with the seeming confusion in their own writings regarding the sufferings of Christ and His glory to follow. It is no surprise that we also fail to fully grasp some biblical teaching. We simply need to believe God's Word and continue prayerful study of the Scriptures.

If we live with the three truths just mentioned, we will be well on our way to sweet fellowship with God and a lifetime of spiritual and emotional stability.

How does knowing the truths taught in the Bible contribute to our fellowship with God?

1. The Bible is God's revelation of His nature and personality.

Revelation is the opposite of reason, when it comes to the discovery of truth. Some truth or at least the probability of it, can be ascertained through logic and experimentation. Some truth however, could never be discovered by human effort or intelligence; it could only be unveiled by God Himself. The fact that God exists is rational, because the creation exists. It must have been caused by someone or something outside of itself. Creation operates by laws, so there must be a lawgiver. The creation has a marvelous design – who designed it? Any honest observer would recognize the existence of God. Only a fool would deny it. On the other hand, the character of God could only be known through revelation. Some might imagine him as a god of wickedness, hatred and evil. Thankfully, God is righteous, loving, just and holy, but reason alone could not justify any conclusion of what God is like. How grateful we can be that God has revealed His attributes in the Bible. Thereby we can know Him and trust Him. This truth provides a basis for communion with Him.

2. The Bible unveils God's plan for time and eternity.

When we are aware of what God is doing, we can understand how to best serve him and be a co-laborer in His cause. We can also grasp what is taking place in our times and therefore know how to live in the current age.

3. The Bible is God's primary method of communicating to us.

Being a born again Christian is wonderful, but we need to hear from God. While there are personal aspects to God's communication to us, such as ministering to us through our conscience to give us peace and conviction, even these must be evaluated by biblical teaching. Amazingly, God has given one book for all people of all time. Studying it and believing what it says, reveals that some of it is directed to certain people and other parts to other people, but all of it will be used by God to educate us and teach us. II Timothy 2:15 gives us clear instruction in regard to these things. Paul wrote, "Study to show thyself approved unto God, a workman that needeth not to be ashamed, rightly dividing the Word of truth."

With these truths in mind, all of us must give thought to how we will equip ourselves with a working knowledge of the Bible, and a living faith, whereby we can employ Bible truth to guide us through life.

Read the Bible with understanding.

It is essential for Christian men to spend time reading the Bible. Women seem to spend more time in the Word than men. Reading the Bible with understanding will require a basic grasp of the groups of the books of Scripture. Maybe the following will help.

Recognize that the first 5 books of the Bible, from Genesis to Deuteronomy are known as the Pentateuch. They record for us the first 2500 years of human history. They include the story of creation, the flood of Noah's day, the establishment of the nations generally, the establishment of the Nation of Israel specifically, and the foundational covenants God made with mankind.

The next 12 books, from Joshua to Esther, give the continuing history of Israel, covering a period of about 1,000 years.

The next 5 books are known as the Poetic books, which include the treasured books of the Psalms and Proverbs.

Following the Poetic books are the 17 books of Old Testament Prophecy. These books coincide with the 12 historical books, since the prophetic writers lived during the years of Israel's historical record. The 5 longest books from Isaiah to Daniel are the Major Prophets. The 12 shorter books from Hosea to Malachi are the Minor Prophets. The terms major and minor are only related to the lengths of the books, not the messages they give. The last of the prophetic books (Malachi) is dated at about 397 BC.

Four hundred years after the close of the Old Testament, God sent John the Baptist to the people of Israel to prepare them for the coming of Jesus Christ. The first 4 books of the New Testament are the Gospels. Those books record the ministry and death of John the Baptist and most significantly, record the birth, ministry, death and resurrection of the Lord Jesus Christ. There are 4 different gospels, because they each give a unique perspective on Christ. Matthew presents him as king, Mark as a servant, Luke as a man and John as deity.

Next comes the book of "The Acts of the Apostles", the single historical book of the New Testament, dealing with the beginning and early ministry of the Church, the spiritual body of Christ. This book must be read carefully, because 4 groups of people are gradually brought into the single body of the Church. The groups include the Jews, the Gentiles, the Samaritans and the early disciples of John the Baptist. Many have fallen into confusion by ignoring the unique qualities and needs of these groups as they were brought to unity in the Church. Be careful!

Following the book of Acts are the 21 New Testament Epistles (letters). These were written to New Testament Church believers by Paul, Peter, James, John and Jude. Each one is worthy of careful study, and the book of Hebrews needs special attention. The recipients of that letter were professing Jews, who in the midst of pressure and persecution were considering a return to Jewish Law and practice. The warnings given in the book address their unique problems, but cannot properly be understood outside of the context of the book and the people who received it. Many have concluded that Hebrews teaches that a believer can lose his salvation, but only by removing a text from its proper context could anyone develop such an erroneous view.

The final book of the New Testament is the incredible "Revelation of Jesus Christ". It is the only New Testament book devoted to prophecy, though other books also have some prophetic teaching.

As we read the Scripture we must remember that every book is for us, but not every book was written to us. I encourage you to read, read, read. Some people read the Bible completely every single year. Others do not, but wise Christians realize they need to read the Book of Books with regularity and understanding. Again I emphasize, the Bible is God's Word speaking to us.

Reading and studying the Bible will reveal principles by which to live

There are many dos and don'ts in Scripture. We must give heed to them, but there are not enough to fully guide us through life. Thankfully, the Bible gives us principles for living that will guide us in facing many of life's challenges, as well as answering many of life's questions. A few are listed, but find more as you read and study.

I Corinthians 10:31 – *Whether therefore ye eat, or drink, or whatsoever ye do, do all to the glory of God.*

I Thessalonians 5:22 – *Abstain from all appearance of evil.*

Romans 13:14b – *...make not provision for the flesh to fulfill the lusts thereof.*

Proverbs 27:2a – *Let another man praise thee, and not thine own mouth...*

Proverbs 20:24 – *Man's goings are of the LORD; how can a man then understand his own way.*

Galatians 6:7b - ...*whatsoever a man soweth, that shall he also reap.*

Reading and studying the Bible will reveal promises we can claim.

It is important to realize that not every promise in Scripture is for us as New Testament believers, especially some in the Old Testament, which were given specifically for the nation of Israel. At the same time, there are many New Testament promises, as well as many in the Old Testament, that we can claim with confidence. It is not hard to distinguish these things as we read the context in which promises are given. Listed are a few precious promises that every man can and should claim for his daily life.

Proverbs 3:5-6 – *Trust in the LORD with all thine heart; and lean not unto thine own understanding. In all thy ways acknowledge him and he shall direct thy paths.*

I Corinthians 10:13 – *There hath no temptation taken you but such as is common to man: but God is faithful, who will not suffer you to be tempted above that ye are able, but will with the temptation also may a way to escape, that ye may be able to bear it.*

Romans 10:13 – *For whosoever shall call upon the name of the Lord shall be saved.*

Hebrews 13:5b – *...for he hath said, I will never leave thee nor forsake thee.*

James 4:7b – *Resist the devil, and he will flee from you.*

Romans 8:26 – *Likewise the Spirit also helpeth our infirmities: for we know not what we should pray for as we ought: but the*

Spirit itself maketh intercession for us with groanings which cannot be uttered.

Acts 1:11 - *...Ye men of Galilee, why stand ye gazing up into heaven? This same Jesus, which is taken up from you into heaven, shall so come in like manner as ye have seen him go into heaven.*

John 14:2-3 – *In my Father's house are many mansions: if it were not so, I would have told you. I go to prepare a place for you. And if I go to prepare a place for you, I will come again and receive you unto myself; that where I am there ye may be also.*

Through the Bible we can learn the ways and character of God.

To say the least, many people, including Christians, have misconceptions about God. We need not, cannot not and should not speculate on these things when we have the very Word of God in our hands. A few verses are listed to introduce God, as he is.

I Corinthians 1:9a – *God is faithful...*

Malachi 3:6a – *I am the LORD, I change not...*

I John 1:9 – *If we confess our sins, he is faithful and just to forgive us our sins and to cleanse us from all unrighteousness.*

II Corinthians 1:3 – *Blessed be God, even the Father of our Lord Jesus Christ, the Father of mercies, and the God of all comfort.*

Psalm 86:15 – *But thou, O LORD, art a God full of compassion, and gracious, longsuffering, and plenteous in mercy and truth.*

Psalm 103:11 – *For as the heaven is high above the earth, so great is his mercy toward them that fear him.*

Mark 10:27b - *...with God all things are possible.*

Titus 1:2 – *In hope of eternal life, which God that cannot lie, promised before the world began...*

The Bible is inexhaustible. The more we learn, the more we realize how little we know. The Apostle Paul told Timothy in II Timothy 2:15, "Study to show thyself approved unto God, a workman that needeth not to be ashamed, rightly dividing the Word of truth." You will never be the man God wants you to be unless you soak yourself in the truths of God's Word. Being in a good church will be of immeasurable value, but your personal reading and study will become a delight as you learn and grow as a Christian.

Chapter 12

Even Deeper Fellowship Through Prayer

As New Testament believers we have an incredible third privilege of fellowship available to us. God has extended to us the moment by moment ongoing invitation to step before His Throne of Grace and speak directly to Him. The Bible calls it prayer. We can praise Him, thank Him, confess to Him, make requests for ourselves, or intercede for others. Unfortunately, for whatever reason, we do not pray enough.

The prayer experience is easy to understand. The Father is on the Throne. The son, our Lord Jesus Christ, is seated next to the Throne. This is the picture given to us in Hebrews 8:1 and Hebrews 10:12 and a number of other places. While on earth, the Lord Jesus explained how prayer would work after He got to heaven. In John 16:23, He said, "And in that day, ye shall ask me nothing. Verily, verily, I say unto you, whatsoever ye shall ask the Father in my name, He will give it you." In verse 26, He affirmed his message again when He said, "At that day ye shall ask in my name…" When we pray we talk to the Father. When we talk to Him, we approach Him in the name "authority" of our Lord Jesus. This picture of prayer is completed by what the Apostle Paul tells us in Romans 8:26-27. There he tells us, the Holy Spirit intercedes for us when we pray, because we do not know exactly what we should request. The Spirit presents our burden in a way that is acceptable to God. So, here it is again; when we pray, we talk to the Father in the name of Jesus Christ. We can fully open our heart to Him, but as we do, the Holy Spirit takes our burdens (which we may not express very well) and lays them perfectly before the Throne of Grace. Prayer is a wonderful experience that offers us hope and encouragement we can only find in talking to God.

The so called "bottom line" of prayer is this. **If I ask God to do something He is willing to do; He will do it.** If I don't ask, there is no reason to think or hope that he will do it. My favorite encouragement to pray is found in Matthew 8:1-3. It says, *When he (Jesus) was come down from the mountain, great multitudes followed him. And, behold, there came a leper and worshipped him, saying, Lord, if thou wilt, thou canst make me clean. And Jesus put forth his hand, and touched him, saying, I will; be thou clean. And immediately his leprosy was cleansed.*

Every time I think about the experience of the leper, I get stirred in my own prayer life. His request was very simple. He told the Lord that he knew, if Jesus wilt (was willing) he could make him clean. Jesus said he was willing, so he reached out and healed him. This amazing experience presents a simple pattern for us. If he is willing – there is no end to what might occur in our lives and the lives of our loved ones, if we pray. That is how I pray. I hope you will pray that way too, because it makes prayer very spiritually exciting. I have no reason to believe the Lord Jesus would have healed the man of his Leprosy, if the man had not asked. I wonder what he has not yet done for you. Ask! So what else is involved in this adventure known as praying?

First, we need to make sure there is nothing in the way. Psalm 66:18 says, *If I regard iniquity in my heart, the Lord will not hear me.* Thankfully, 1 John 1:9 says, *If we confess our sins, he is faithful and just to forgive our sins and to cleanse us from all unrighteousness.* Now this is serious. The word confess means, to say the same thing, so true confession is us saying about our sin what God says – and turning from it. God will forgive us, and that puts us on praying ground.

Second, we must realize that our request must be in harmony with what God is willing to do. He is not going to contradict his own character or his Word, nor can we expect him to accommodate our greediness, selfishness or vengeance. Aside from those rather obvious issues, we find great hope in 1 John 5:14-15. *And this is the confidence that we have in him, that, if we ask anything according to his will (willingness), he heareth us. And if we know that he hears us, whatsoever we ask, we know we have the petitions that we desired of him.* You and I don't know what God might be willing to do. James told his readers in 4:3 of his letter, "ye have not, because ye ask not." What might God do, if we ask?

Third, we rest in God's ability to do whatever He is willing to do. I love Ephesians 3:20-21. *Now unto him, who is able to do exceeding abundantly above all that we ask or think, according to the power that worketh in us, unto him be glory in the church by Christ Jesus throughout all ages, world without end. Amen.* Don't miss the message of these verses. Paul says God is able, and his ability exceeds what we might dare to ask or even think. Are you ignoring the possibilities of prayer?

Make this experience personal and spiritually intimate. What do we mean by that? Keep much of your prayer life secret. There are times we might ask others to pray about a matter and that is fine. Paul certainly sought the prayer support of others. At the same time, consider the words of our Lord Jesus in Matthew 6:6. He said, *But when thou prayest, enter into thy closet, and when thou hast shut the door, pray to thy Father which is in secret; and thy Father which seeth in secret shall reward thee openly.* Learn to love the secret place. There we can share with our heavenly Father the burdens, feelings, struggles and desires that we could never tell another person. Remember to think of God as *Abba Father.* This Aramaic term used of a small child personally addressing his own father. It suggests perfect trust and confidence such as only a little one might find in his daddy. That kind of trust and confidence is what we can have as we approach God in prayer. Finally, keep asking. You can turn to the parable in Luke 18:1-8 and read it for encouragement. Verse 1 makes the purpose of the parable very clear. *And he spake a parable unto them to this end, that men ought always to pray, and not to faint.* Faint means to lose heart. If you are burdened for a matter, keep praying, don't give up. Sometimes God says no, because He has something better in mind; sometimes He says wait. Our job, as the song writer put it is, - keep on praying til the light breaks through.

Praying deepens our fellowship with God in amazing ways. It is very personal, and when we see God respond, we will be drawn closer and closer to him.

Here is an invitation found in the book of Hebrews. It is based on the fact that the Lord Jesus is a faithful high priest, who understands our needs and burdens. Hebrews 4:16, *Let us therefore come boldly unto the throne of grace, that we may obtain mercy, and find grace to help in time of need.* The term "boldly" means with confidence.

Here is a great invitation given by the Lord Jesus in Matthew 7:7-11. He said, *Ask and it shall be given unto you; seek and ye shall find; knock and it shall be opened unto you: For everyone that asketh receiveth; and he that seeketh findeth; and to him that knocketh, it shall be opened. Or what man is there of you, whom if his son ask bread, will he give him a stone? Or if he ask for a fish, will he give him a serpent? If ye then, being evil, know how to give good gifts unto your children, how much more shall your Father which is in heaven give good things to them that ask him?*

There is certainly more to prayer than we have covered in this chapter, but I encourage you to take advantage of the opportunity to talk personally with the God that created us. It is no bother to him. He wants us to pray. He cares about our burdens and He is the one who has the power to do something about them.

Chapter 13

Sanctification – the Spirit and the Body

As Christian men, we are expected to grow and change as we move ahead in life. Peter exhorted the readers of his letters with that challenge. In I Peter 2:2 he wrote, *As newborn babes, desire the sincere milk of the Word, that ye may **grow** thereby*. He closed his second letter by saying, *But **grow** in the grace and knowledge of our Lord and Savior Jesus Christ. To him be glory both now and forever. Amen*. Paul complimented the believers at Thessalonica in 1:3 of his second letter saying, *We are bound to thank God always for you, brethren as it is meet, because your faith **growth** exceedingly*. On the other hand, Hebrews 5:12 chides believers by saying, *For when for the time ye ought to be teachers, ye have need that one teach you again…* They had not grown. There are many aspects to growing and changing, however, I have found I Thessalonians 5:23 to be most meaningful in understanding the challenge. Paul wrote**, And the very God of peace sanctify you wholly; and I pray God your whole spirit and soul and body be preserved blameless unto the coming of our Lord Jesus Christ."** This text verse is very significant. Follow its message carefully.

Paul begins by referring to God as the "God of peace". He uses that title because he is going to show us the pathway to real peace, and we desperately need peace in our hearts and our minds. God reveals himself through many names and titles such as: Father of mercies (II Corinthians 1:3), God of all grace (I Peter 5:10), and God our Savior (Titus 1:3).

In this way He introduces His attributes and how He ministers to us through them. God wants us to have peace and he tells us how to get it.

After introducing God as the God of peace, Paul calls for our complete sanctification. That is the pathway to peace. Sanctification means separation **to God**. Often, separation **from things** is preached. If the message is biblical, that can be a very appropriate challenge, but the key to true sanctification is moving toward God. If we just turn away from a list of wrong things, we will never get wholly sanctified. We could move away from drugs, but still be involved with immoral practices. If we move toward God, we will move away from both the drugs and immorality. Real peace will come to us when we move "wholly" toward God.

To help us understand the process of sanctification, Paul breaks down our being into its three elements – spirit, soul and body. Let's talk about each one.

Spirit:

Our human spirit is the deepest part of our being. The term spirit is sometimes interchanged in the Bible with the term heart. Our spirit gives us God consciousness. When we are born again, the Holy Spirit gives spiritual life to our human spirit. The Lord Jesus said, *That which is born of the Spirit is spirit* (John 3:6). In I Corinthians 6:20, Paul said we are to glorify God in our spirit. In Romans 12:11, Paul talked about being fervent in spirit. Mark 8:12 says our Lord sighed deeply in His spirit, but in Luke 10:21, he rejoiced in spirit. In the Old Testament we find references to a haughty spirit, a humble spirit, and the challenge to rule one's spirit.

In our text, Paul said our spirit needs to be sanctified. Consider what goes on in the deepest part of your being. We all struggle in living for the Lord, but can you say that deep within, you genuinely want to serve Him. The Lord Jesus warned his disciples to watch and pray so they would not enter into temptation, because while their spirit was willing, their flesh was weak (Matthew 26:41). Here is a question. Is your spirit willing? You may mess up a lot, or maybe just a little, but can you honestly say that deep down you truly want to live for God. That is where growing and changing begins. If there is no tenderness for God in our spirit, the road ahead is going to be very hard. What should be sobering is this. While no one else can see what we are in heart and spirit – we know and God knows. Stubbornness and resistance at this level is rebellion at its worst. David knew the depths of his sin when in Psalm 51:10 he cried to God, *Create in me a clean heart and renew a right spirit within me.* There have certainly been times in my life when I knew what I should be, but I could not seem to get there. I knew I needed God to help me. Maybe that is where you are. If so, ask God to work in you – to renew a right spirit within.

Body:

The last area Paul mentioned in I Thessalonians 5:23 is the body, but I want to consider it here, before we talk about the soul. As the spirit gives us God consciousness, the body gives us world consciousness. Without the physical senses of sight, hearing, smell, taste and touch, we would have no awareness of the world around us. Of course, the body has no life in itself. When we die the soul/spirit leaves the body, and the body is dead. Our body is simply the vehicle through which we express outwardly what is going on inwardly. The body does have physical drives however, which often turn to sinful lusts in the inner man. Therefore, Paul tells us we must bring our body into subjection. I Corinthians 9:24-27 tells us we must discipline and train our body. We need to control it, instead of it controlling us. The message of the Corinthian verses compares the athlete's discipline of his body with the need for the Christian to control his body. Paul reminds us the athlete is only vying for a physical crown, but Christians must live with the thought of standing before the judgment seat of Christ. Paul tells us in I Corinthians 6:13 that **the body is for the Lord**, but do we think about that? We have already addressed the challenge to present our body as a living sacrifice to God, as we saw in Romans 12:1-2, but that is only the beginning of a day to day experience of living victoriously for Christ. If the body is for the Lord, I have to control what I see with my eyes, hear with my ears, taste with my tongue, smell with my nose and touch with my hands. All this must be controlled, because as Paul emphasized in I Corinthians 6:20, Christians have been bought by the blood of Christ and are therefore to **glorify God in their body**, as well as in their spirit.

It can be tough to control our body. Too many men are hooked on eating, drinking or drugs. Many more have a difficult time controlling what their eyes see and what their ears hear. Discipline is lacking and immorality abounds among men who testify to being saved. There is no peace when the body is functioning on the basis of lust. The body must be sanctified and the senses must be used to magnify the Lord, not satisfy uncontrolled yearnings. There is no peace when we are addicted to sinful practice. Sin will take you further than you want to go and once you are snared, it is tough to get free.

Chapter 14

The Battle to Sanctify the Soul

The second area Paul mentioned in I Thessalonians 5:23 is the soul. I call it the battle ground of the Christian life. The word translated *soul* is often translated *life* in Scripture. It refers to our natural life. The soul gives us self-consciousness. It includes our mind, emotions, will and conscience. The warfare in these areas is as challenging as anything we will ever face on the outside. I can escape the outside, but my only option is to win on the inside. Let's talk about it.

Mind

The mind involves thinking, understanding and remembering. Have you ever been defeated in those areas? ABSOLUTELY for you and for me. And one thing is sure, we cannot have peace if these things don't change.

I am both conflicted and encouraged that God requires us to accept responsibility for what we think? When Paul talks about the *peace that passeth understanding,* in Philippians 4:7; he immediately, in verse 8, tells us what and how to think. That is the challenge to control our own thinking. God will help, but what a battle it will be. However, we cannot yield to a wandering mind. It will destroy us. How often do you find yourself thinking about the wrong things? Don't tolerate it! Unfortunately, we have lazy minds. We have not disciplined them.

I want that victory and I fight for it every day. How about you? In II Corinthians 10:5 Paul spoke about *casting down imaginations, and every high thing that exalteth itself against the knowledge of God and bringing into captivity every thought to the obedience of Christ.* That is strong action on our part. It means, when we get wrong thoughts (imaginations) we have to pull them down by force to destroy them (casting down). We have to *bring them into captivity* (subjugate and bring under control). Our thinking must be in obedience to Christ.

Then comes memory. Paul said we need to forget those things that are behind (Philippians 3:13), but memory can haunt us and ruin our lives. What a war we are in! Do things you want to forget keep coming into your mind?

What about understanding? In Ephesians 4:18, Paul said that before we were saved our understanding was darkened. We all have views and opinions, but they may not be governed by an understanding of God's truth.

It is no wonder Paul said in Romans 12:2 we need a renewing of our mind. Sanctification of our mind will be achieved when our thinking is under control; we can forget what we ought to forget; and our understanding of all things is being conformed to the teaching of Scripture.

Emotions

Our emotions are also part of the soul. How many men cannot control their feelings? We can get angry, bitter, hateful, malicious and lustful. Sometimes it is sadness, depression or self-pity. Here again, we must not tolerate these failures, but things will not simply change with the passing of time. A great part of our victory in this area can come by forgiving those who have hurt, failed or offended us, because people's ways and words are often the source of these problems. Ephesians 4:31-

32 is helpful. Other times circumstances will take us down. It can be loneliness, financial struggle, sickness or other matters where no other person is involved. In such situations we take appropriate action to solve the problem if possible, but we must also humble ourselves before the Lord. In I Peter 5:6-10, we are given great help, instruction and encouragement. Read these verses. Believe what they say and do what they tell us to do. Emotions are tough. We cannot simply change our feelings with a momentary decision. We must learn to trust the Lord and obey his Word, so we can grow in the ability to find peace in the Lord. Failure here will undermine any testimony for Christ. Get in this battle. Don't be a victim of your thinking or your feelings. It is a terrible way to live, and it will deeply affect your loved ones as well as yourself.

Will

The next aspect of our soul is our will. We are not robots. God has given us the ability to make choices and decisions. Too often we end up with regrets. Maybe we did not have all the information we needed; maybe we were just being stubborn; maybe we got bad advice, but for whatever reason we made the wrong choice. We need to do better. Of course, decision making is greatly affected by our mind and our emotions. We need a biblical/spiritual basis for the choices we make. Good, godly counsel and advice can help. We often must make choices that we don't feel like making, but we do so, because they are right before God. Joshua told the people of Israel to choose who they would serve (Joshua 24:15). Elijah told Israel to get off the fence and make up their minds to serve God (I Kings 18:21). Choosing can be tough, but we need to develop a pattern of making good, godly choices, in spite of internal or external pressures to go the wrong direction. Too often I have talked with men who have made bad choices over and over again. And, whether we like it or not, for the most part we are where we are in life, based on the choices we have made. May God give us wisdom as we go forward.

Conscience

Finally, the soul includes our conscience. The term means, *a knowledge that is with us*, (from *con – with* and (*science – to know*). God has given us an internal knowledge of basic morality. When we go astray the conscience is supposed to judge us and make us feel guilty. This is a wonderful protection which God has put within us to keep us on the right path. Unfortunately, we often defile our conscience by choosing to do or say what we know is wrong. Continually defiling our Conscience can lead to a condition called searing (I Timothy 4:2). That is when we don't feel guilty, even though we should. That is dangerous! I want to feel guilty when God says I should feel guilty.

Here is an added problem. The basic morality within us is rooted in our heart, which is the seat of our values and standards. So what if my heart is messed up? The Bible warns us in Jeremiah 17:9, *The heart is deceitful above all things and desperately wicked: who can know (understand) it?*

What a challenge! There are people who do wrong because they don't care. Their mind and emotions are not working right. There are others who do wrong and have no guilt, because they don't believe what they are doing is wrong. Confused? Conscience is a tough area because the conscience itself can be defiled and seared; and the heart, which gives the conscience its basis for judgment can be perverted by unbiblical standards and values. David knew his only hope in this battle was scripture. He wrote in Psalm 119:11, *Thy word have I hid in my heart, that I might sin against thee.*

We certainly have not exhausted the topic of the soul, but it is easy to see how important it is to have God sanctify our mind, emotions, will and conscience. That is the only way we can grow, and change into the man God wants us to be. David also wrote these words in Psalm 119:7. *Wherewithal shall a young man cleanse his way? By taking heed thereto, according to thy word.* In other words our life will be cleaned up when we measure our ways, by God's Word. Saturate yourself with Scripture and seek to obey it.

We need to grow and change. Think how long you have been saved. What should a man be like, who has been saved as long as you? One thing I know, no matter how much we have grown we all have a long way to go. We cannot afford to stop changing, learning, growing, - being transformed into the image of Christ.

It is easy to become complacent in our Christian walk. We feel satisfied with where we are and have no motivation to climb to higher spiritual ground. Often we fall into the trap of comparing ourselves with others. We see the weak, the unfaithful, the inconsistent, the hypocrite or whoever. Thinking we are just as good as, or even better than them. We have no zeal for God. We become apathetic. There is no passion for spiritual things and no desire to fervently serve the Lord.

Growing spiritually does not just happen. We need to think about where we are compared to where God would want us to be. It has nothing to do with how other people live. Get into this battle.

Setting Appropriate Achievable Goals

By now you may have identified areas in your life that need attention. If so, it is time to set some realistic goals to grow and change, which by God's grace, will prove to be achievable.

Begin by thinking through what circumstances or what people might contribute to your times of difficulty or failure. We have referenced Matthew 26:41, but we come back to it, because it can help us tremendously. The text says, *Watch and pray that ye enter not into temptation, for the spirit indeed is willing, but the flesh is weak.* When the Lord Jesus gave this exhortation to his disciples, He knew they were going to face great pressure through the time of his arrest, trial and crucifixion. He wanted them to be ready.

"Watch" means to be alert, watchful, or vigilant. Too often we stumble over similar circumstances time after time. Do you have times when you are more vulnerable to failure than others? It could be when you are with certain people. It could be when you are alone, and no one is with you or watching. It could be when you are tired or when you are under pressure. Think about it (watch) and be alert to the spiritual or emotional dangers that arise in those situations. The Lord Jesus then said, "Pray". Pray in preparation for those times, so you are ready to fight that battle. Ask the Lord to help you guard your mind, words and actions in those settings. Ask Him to give you wisdom in responding to whatever might occur. Ask Him to help you learn the lessons He has in mind for you. Ask Him to help you focus on the fact that people are not our real enemies. Our real battle is spiritual – and Satan and his emissaries are the ones who seek to destroy us. Remember that the Lord acknowledged; *the spirit is willing* (I hope yours is), *but the flesh is weak* (I know yours is – so is mine).

Another text that is helpful is Romans 13:14. *But put ye on the Lord Jesus Christ, and make not provision for the flesh to fulfill the lusts thereof.* This is a verse we have mentioned earlier, but let's emphasize its importance here. We cannot always avoid the wrong people or the wrong circumstances, but when we can, it can be a good thing. If we intentionally get into situations where we know we may say or do the wrong thing, we are making provision for the flesh.

With the message of Matthew 26:41 and Romans 13:14 in mind, I encourage you to set some spiritual and emotional goals in the following areas. We are not going to be perfect, but we need to do better. List some issues of concern under the headings given below and put down what you need to do to improve.

Personal life –

    1.

    2.

    3.

Family life –

    1.

    2.

    3.

Friends & Friendships -

1.

2.

3.

Reputation in your community -

1.

2.

3.

Church faithfulness and service -

1.

2.

3.

Professional life –

1.

2.

3.

So, what are you going to do – or stop doing?

Beyond what we just mentioned we need to consider character qualities which affect all the areas mentioned above.

Carefully consider the characteristics listed below and grade yourself on the positive ones with: A B C D or F. The positive quality is matched with a negative attribute to help you think about an appropriate grade. Some may not seem as important to you as others, but all these characteristics tell the story of our life and testimony before God and others. Each of the ones selected is important, though the list amounts to less than half of the characteristics we might mention. If you are not sure what grade to give yourself, you might dare to ask your wife, children or a friend to give you their opinions. Of course, THAT COULD BE TOUGH. If you decide to keep it to yourself, try to see yourself as others might see you. So, where are you on the following?

Truthfulness vs. Deceptiveness   _____

Virtue vs. Immorality   _____

Self – Control vs. Undisciplined   _____

Joyfulness vs. Distress   _____

Generosity vs. Miserliness   _____

Endurance vs. Weakness   _____

Reverence vs. Disrespect   _____

Diligence vs. Laziness   _____

Dependability vs. Unreliability   _____

Patience vs. Frustration   _____

Discernment vs. Gullibility   _____

Discretion vs. Foolishness   _____

Faith vs. Unbelief   _____

Sincerity vs. Hypocrisy   _____

Gratefulness vs. Pride   _____

Responsibility vs. Neglectfulness   _____

Courage vs. Cowardice   _____

Determination vs. Wavering   _____

Loyalty vs. Disloyalty   _____

Compassion vs. Indifference   _____

Politeness vs. Rudeness   _____

Attentiveness vs. Disregard   _____

Don't be satisfied with a "C". We are supposed to be Christ-like. Character is not so much what we do. It is what we are, and what we are, will determine what we do. Based on your own assessment of yourself, do you need to change? Are you willing to change? Through the power of the Holy Spirit, study of God's Word and prayer, you can begin true growth and change, leading to a transformation of your life.

Chapter 16

Practical Living for Christ

If any man wants to live for God, there are practical things that need to be part of his life. Let's talk about the day to day experience of living for God.

Get baptized

You need to be baptized. We should be baptized as soon as possible after we are saved. The term *baptize* means to immerse or dip. God ordained baptism as a unique way to testify that we have come to know Christ as our savior. It is done by being immersed backward in water. It is a picture of death, burial and resurrection. It shows what has happened to us spiritually when we put our faith in Christ. In Acts 8, Phillip explained the gospel of Christ to a servant of Candace the Queen of Ethiopia. Phillip must have even taught him about being baptized, because we read in Acts 8:36 -37 the following words. *And as they went on their way, they came unto a certain water: and the eunuch (servant) said; See here is water; what doth hinder me to be baptized. And Phillip said; If thou believest with all thine heart thou mayest. And he answered and said, I believe that Jesus Christ is the Son of God.* The text goes on to say that the men went down into the water and the man was baptized (immersed). Baptism does not save us or make us any more saved. It tells everyone, we are saved. **You need to be baptized**. Sure, you can tell people you are saved by other means – and you should, but baptism is specified by God as a step every Christian should take. Baptism is an ordinance God entrusted to local churches. Talk to your pastor if you have no yet been baptized. Now is the time.

Clear the past

Even after we are saved we continue to sin in various ways. We certainly want to grow, and live a righteous and godly life, so we need to confess our sin daily and be sure there is nothing between us and the Lord. We also want to do our best to be sure there is nothing between us and people. Sometimes there are things, even from the distant past, that need to be addressed. I want to be careful here because I am not suggesting that we go back and try to rewrite history. When we are saved, God forgives us and wipes the slate clean. What I have in mind by clearing the past can be illustrated by an experience I had with a young believer. A man got saved through our church ministry. Before he was saved, he had a court order to make certain payments. He ignored them and moved out of the area. When he got saved he felt compelled to go back and make things right, even though he feared arrest. I told him I would go with him. We went, not knowing whether he would return with me or be immediately held by the court. Without going into all the detail, he shared with authorities how he had gotten saved and that he wanted to make things right. The whole matter was cleared and he was free – free from the courts and free within his own heart. It may be that you want to live for Christ, but there is something in the past that must be made right. Get good godly counsel before you take any steps, but don't live haunted by some unresolved matters that could hinder your testimony for Christ. Some things can be handled with a phone call or a note. Sometimes there may be a financial price to pay, but do your best to clear the past. AGAIN, I SAY, get good godly counsel before taking any steps.

Magnify the Lord

The Apostle Paul wrote in I Corinthains 10:31, "Whether therefore ye eat, or drink, or whatsoever ye do, do all to the glory of God". To bring glory to God is a powerful life principle. It will not "just happen". It will come through determination to magnify God in everything we say or do. Think of it this way. Your life as a Christian will affect how people view God. Once we let people know we are saved and that we represent God, as ambassadors for Christ (II Corinthians 5:20), they are going to judge God by what they see in our life. We have to think about how we can honor God and draw people to him, by how we live. That does not mean we compromise on principle or refuse to stand for the truth, for fear someone will get offended. Many times the truth will anger people. We cannot change that, but our attitude and spirit are important. We need to find the balance. People may stumble over the truth, but we don't want our words or ways to be the cause of their rejection of the Lord. In Philippians 1:20, Paul said his expectation and hope was that Christ would be magnified in his body. That is what we should have as our constant desire.

Get into the Scriptures

I don't know how much you know about the Bible, but it is the message of God to us. I have been studying it and preaching it for over 50 years. The more I study, the more I realize that the depth of its truth and the depth of its teaching is inexhaustible. I love it. I ask God to help me understand it. I am going to encourage you to be faithful in attendance at a good church, but at this point I want you to know that you will not get enough from church or Bible studies. You need to read the Bible and let God open your heart and mind to what He has for you. Going to a good church will help you learn true doctrine and avoid false teaching. That is absolutely necessary. Reading for yourself will allow the Spirit of God to take truth to the depths of your heart and mind. Normally in life we say, begin at the beginning. In Bible reading we usually say, do not begin at the beginning. Don't get me wrong, Genesis gives us the wonderful story of Creation and so much more, so you might enjoy it and profit from it. However for spiritual growth and practical wisdom I am going to suggest you begin by investing time in three books of the Bible. Proverbs is a book of practical wisdom for living. There are 31 chapters in the book. With 7 months having 31 days, it gives you a chapter a day. For the other months you will have to double for a few days. Proverbs will challenge, teach you and bless you. The second book I suggest is the Gospel of John. This book presents Jesus Christ as our God and Savior. It only has 21 chapters. You will be in awe as you read about our Lord. The third book is Romans. It was written by the Apostle Paul and lays out clearly the wonderful message of Salvation. Read these books; then read them again; then again. As you read, ask God to open your understanding, so you can grasp the message of the passage you are reading. Don't "read into" the Bible. Let it tell you God's story. You will be blessed. Of course, there are 63 other books of the Bible and every one of them worthy of our study and devotion.

Confess and forsake

I remember being encouraged as a young believer to "keep short accounts with God". We all sin as Christians, but the hope, as we grow, is that our sins will become less and less serious, and that we will deal with them as quickly as possible. Thankfully, some sins end virtually the moment we get saved. As a teenager, and member of the local volunteer fire company, I drank alcohol. After I got saved, I never took another drink. I could wish other sins disappeared as fast, but gradually we grow and change. So what do we do when we sin? Proverbs 28:13 offers wonderful encouragement. It says, *He that covereth his sins shall not prosper, but whoso confesseth and forsaketh them shall have mercy.* To *confess* means to agree with God about my sin. I say about it what He says. Obviously, *forsake* means to turn from it and stop doing it. If I let sin linger in my heart and life, it will get worse. God warns us in Psalm 66:18, *If I regard iniquity in my heart, the Lord will not hear me.* I need God to hear me when I pray. I need His help and guidance, so I don't want to risk losing His blessing. Of course, pride gets in the way, and we do not like to admit we do wrong. If we are wise however, we will identify sin for what it is, confess to God when we fail, and take the steps necessary to walk away from it. It can be hard at first, but living for him will get easier the more we do it. In Romans 12:9, Paul told us to, *Abhor that which is evil; cleave to that which is good.* Believe me – it gets better and better as we live for Him.

Handle problems biblically

This is a challenge that most – yes most, Christians ignore. We are not going to exhaust this topic in this brief paragraph, but if you get hold of some basics, you will save yourself and others a lot of trouble and heartache. Let's begin with Matthew 18:15. The Lord Jesus said, *Moreover if thy brother shall trespass against thee, go and tell him his fault between he and thee alone: if he shall hear thee, thou hast gained thy brother.* The challenge is to talk to this person alone. (Get some pastoral guidance if the offender is a young person or of the opposite gender). The emphasis of the teaching is **ALONE.** Don't tell other people. It is a powerful testimony to go to a person and be able to say – **I have not talked to any other person about this.** This is biblical, and it offers the greatest hope for solving the problem. You can be firm, but be gracious, and see what God might do. Another teaching comes from Paul in Ephesians 4:31-32. He wrote, *Let all bitterness, and wrath, and anger, and clamor, and evil speaking, be put away from you, with all malice: And be ye kind one to another, tenderhearted, forgiving one another, even as God,* *for Christ's sake hath forgiven you.* Many Christians get terribly defeated through bitterness, wrath, anger etc. Don't let that be you. Determine to forgive your offenders. Most will not come back to seek forgiveness, so don't wait for it. Reconciliation is wonderful, but sometimes impossible. We forgive by making a decision to turn the offender over to the Lord. The Bible says vengeance belongs to Him. When we turn the matter over to Him, we can get spiritually and emotionally free. God always does the right thing. We can rest in that. Forgiveness is wiping the slate clean. Paul tells us to forgive even as God for Christ sake hath forgiven us. We don't deserve forgiveness, but God gives it to us, to honor what Christ did in dying for us on the cross. The person who hurt us may not "deserve" forgiveness, but we forgive to also honor the work of Christ on the cross. Of course the Bible has much more to say about problem solving, but these two instructions will bring incredible blessing to your life. Offences and hurts will come. How we handle them will be critical in determining how successful we are in our walk with Christ.

Chapter 17

More Practical Living for Christ

Worship faithfully

Begin to worship God in a way that truly honors Him. The biblical term for worship is a contraction of two words. One means "forward" and the other "to kiss". It translates into the idea of reverence and obeisance. Our English word "worship" comes from an Old English term meaning to "ascribe worth". It is obvious then that we can "worship God"in a variety of ways, and we should. We must also realize that the Lord has prescribed a primary way for believers to worship as a group. The major work being carried on by God in this age was expressed by the Lord Jesus in Matthew 16:18, where he said, *I will build my church.* The word Church means "called out ones". When you got saved, God called you out from this wicked world system. The church is a spiritual **organism**. It is the body, and Christ is the head. Christ is not only the head of the church however, He is also called the Good Shepherd (John 10:11), the Great Shepherd (Hebrews 13:20), and the Chief Shepherd (I Peter 5:4). He is the shepherd; we are the sheep. To fulfill this role the Lord established an **organization**. To care for the sheep He has appointed shepherds. The term we find in our Bible is Pastor, which means shepherd. The whole church body cannot meet together, but God's people congregate in local churches. Each one has a shepherd (Pastor). But there is also further structure to the local church laid out in Scripture. There are deacons who assist the Pastor. (Ephesians 4:11,

I Timothy 3:1-13) The church meets on the first day of the week for preaching, fellowship, financial giving and prayer (I Corinthians 16:1, Acts 20:7). The local church sends and supports missionaries (Acts 13:1-4). The church disciplines believers who choose a pathway of sin and immorality (I Corinthians 5:1-5). The local church baptizes and provides the fellowship of the Lord's table (Acts 18:8, I Corinthians 11:17-34). Why do we say all these things? Because this is God's plan for this age. I encourage you to find a good local church that teaches and follows the Bible. Worship the Lord in church and endeavor to be faithful every time the doors are open.

Find ways to serve

When we get saved we are called to serve the Lord. Psalm 100:2 says *Serve the Lord with gladness...* Colossians 3:24 says, *Ye serve the Lord Christ.* Paul commended the Christians in I Thessalonians 1:9 for turning *from idols to serve the living God.* Have you found ways to serve? Faithfully attending a good local church is the beginning of service to the Lord, but it is only the beginning. You might serve in simple ways like greeting visitors or receiving the offering. But there is more. You might get into the technical aspects of sound and video. You might go on visits to new attendees, unbelievers, sick or homebound. You might work with the youth, teach a Bible Study or a Sunday School class. Perhaps you would feel better equipped to mow grass, clean a building, do maintenance or work on vehicles. The time could come that you would go on a missions trip or help at camp outings or retreats. How about joining the choir or playing an instrument. Maybe you will be elected to be a church officer. There is really no end to the possibilities. Start praying, and start seeking opportunities to invest your time, energies and talents in the work of the Lord at your local church. It will be fruitful and meaningful. The Lord will bless you and use you for His glory.

Establish a public testimony

Psalm 107:2 begins with these words, *Let the redeemed of the LORD say so.* One of the best things we can do as believers is to let people know that we are born again Christians. For one thing, it will establish a measure of accountability for ourselves. When we publicly identify with our Savior, we will be mindful that our words and ways will reflect on Him. When King David sinned with Bathsheba, he was confronted by the prophet Nathan. The prophet's words were extremely convicting. He said, *by this deed thou hast given great occasion to the enemies of the LORD to blaspheme.* That is the last thing we want to do. I don't want to be someone else's excuse for mocking and refusing God. Another reason why establishing a public testimony is that we want people to know that our godly testimony is not because we are just nice people or even religious people. We want them to know that Jesus Christ has transformed our lives. A third reason to establish a public testimony is the fact that it can save you a lot of trouble. I enjoy playing golf (though I am not too good at it), but on the golf course you will meet all kinds of people. Unfortunately, some of them may have a pretty foul mouth, especially if they hit a bad shot. I try, as quickly as possible, to get a word out for the Lord. It usually brings a halt to the bad language, and can open great opportunities to present the gospel. Don't worry about being labeled as the guy who got religion, or being called "deacon" or whatever. It will be worth it. Also, guys who may be rather vile will know who to look for when they face hard times. We don't have to be forceful, pushy, arrogant or condemning. Also we don't need to worry about being able to answer every theological or biblical question we might be asked. All we have to do is what Jesus Christ told the man he delivered from demonic power in Mark 5:19, *Go home to thy friends, and tell them how great things the Lord hath done for thee, and hath had compassion on thee.* Follow that simple instruction – you can't go wrong.

Seek the lost

Most of us are familiar with what is commonly known as the Great Commission. It is recorded in Matthew 28:18-20; Mark 16:15-18; Luke 24:46-53; and Acts 1:8. Based on the simple truth that Jesus said He had come to seek and to save the lost; He commands believers of this age to take the Gospel to every person. Some are called by God to "full time" service. That typically means a man leaves secular employment, studies the Word of God formally, and is supported by other Christians to teach and preach the gospel in his own Country or a foreign nation. Probably more have been called to do that then are actually doing it. Even so, such a call seems reserved for a relatively small percentage of Christians. If God calls you – GO. On the other hand, every believer should be involved in evangelism. Are you trying to reach people for Christ? I would encourage you to make a list of prospective people, who you might be able to reach in some way. Start with immediate family and then go on to extended family. Next think about friends and neighbors. Move on to work acquaintances. Then there might be a number of people who are outside of those circles. With that simple approach, how many unsaved people are on the list? What are you going to do about them? There are many ways to evangelize. Personally talking to someone is best, but we can give gospel tracts, write letters, or maybe invite people to church services or Bible studies. Begin to pray for people on your list and ask the Lord to give you an opportunity to tell them about Christ.

Tithes and offerings

One of the most exciting things we can do to serve the Lord, is to financially support God's work. The main way God established for giving is the tithe. "Tithe" is the translation of both Hebrew and Greek words that mean "tenth". God required the people of Israel to bring their tithes to the Temple, but long before there was a Temple, Abraham paid tithes in Genesis 14:20, to Melchizedek, Priest of the Most High God. When the Church began, believers no longer had obligation to the Jewish Temple. They gave to their local Church.

The tithe is our way of testifying our recognition that all we have was provided by the gracious hand of God. The prophet Malachi told the Jews who refused to bring their tithes to the Temple, they were actually robbing God. Since I got saved I have given one tenth of my gross income to the Lord. I believe God has blessed me and my family because of our acknowledgement that everything we have received in life is from Him.

Depending on your age, marital status and financial circumstances, you may not tithe and may not think you can afford it. I encourage you to begin immediately, because I believe with Malachi, that to keep that tenth of our income for our use would be to rob God. I believe we live better on the 90% that is left over after tithing, than we would live on the 100% we would have if we don't tithe. The Prophet Haggai told the non-tithing Jews of his day that their refusal to honor God financially would put them in a situation where getting their wages would be like putting their money in a bag with a holes. I have always interpreted that as Haggai saying, "God may not get what he deserves from you, but you are not going to get it either". Some will think God is being unfair, but wait, do you think you would have ANYTHING, if God did not provide it? God blesses us for giving, far beyond what we might ever deserve. The tithe should go to our local church? Some want to take their tithe and give to other people or other ministries. The Bible says, the tithe is the Lord's. The best way to give it to Him is to get it out of our hands and out of our control. The Lord started the Church. It is His work in this age. Give your tithe to the Church. If you want to give more than your tithe, give offerings above your tithe, to people or other ministries in the Lord's name. Let me emphasize, we are not under Jewish Law and thereby required to tithe. As we mentioned, tithing was practiced long before the Law was instituted. It stands as a testimony to our thanksgiving to God for all he has given to us.

Final Thoughts

Many thoughts come to mind as we close this book, but I am reminded specifically of Paul's words from II Corinthians 5:10. He said, *For we must all appear before the judgment seat of Christ; that everyone may receive the things done in his body, according to that he hath done, whether it be good or bad.*

Someday each one of us will stand personally before Jesus Christ at what is called, the judgment seat. That judgment is only for believers and will not determine if a person will go to heaven. It is a judgment at which we will *appear.* The term *appear* means to be manifest. I Corinthians 4:5 expresses it beautifully. *Therefore judge nothing before the time, until the Lord come, who both will **bring to light the hidden things of darkness, and will make manifest the counsels of the hearts;** and then shall every man have praise of God.* In simple words, it means the real you and the real me will be put on public display for all to see. The secret sins and the wicked heart will be exposed. It is no wonder John warns us in I John 2:28, *And now little children, abide in him; that when he shall appear, we may have confidence, and not be ashamed before him at his coming.*

I don't want to be ashamed before Christ when I stand in front of him. That means I cannot be a shallow phony now. I cannot play games with God and I cannot be a hypocrite before the world or other Christians.

The judgment seat is intended to be a place of reward, not shame. However, Paul addressed this matter in I Corinthians 3:11-15. He said,

For other foundation can no man lay than that is laid, which is Jesus Christ. Now if any man build upon this foundation gold, silver, precious stones; wood, hay stubble; every man's work shall be made manifest: for the day shall declare it, because it shall be revealed by fire; and the fire shall try every man's work, of what sort it is. If any man's work abide which he hath built thereupon, he shall receive a reward. If any man's work shall be burned, he shall suffer loss: but he himself shall be saved; yet so as by fire.

These verses present quite a picture. When we got saved we laid a new foundation for our very existence, and that foundation was Christ. It was the beginning of a new life. From the day of our salvation until the day we die we build our testimony for Christ. Paul likens it to building a structure using either good solid materials (a strong genuine testimony for Christ) or weak tenuous materials (a shallow worldly walk). When our life ends our "building" will be tested by fire. The fire of judgment will consume our worthless ways and actions. Anything of spiritual and eternal worth will be preserved and rewarded.

This is the message of the verse we started with in II Corinthians 5:10. In that judgment, a man will *receive the things done in his body, according to that he hath done, whether it be good or bad (worthless).*

Does all this matter? It mattered to the Lord Jesus who told His disciples in Matthew 6:19-21, *Lay not up for yourselves treasures upon earth, where moth and rust doth corrupt, and where thieves break through and steal, but lay up for yourselves treasures in heaven, where neither moth nor rust doth corrupt, and where thieves do not break through nor steal; for where your treasure is, there will your heart be also.*

The rewards to be received are described as crowns. The term for crown speaks of a reward given for victory in conflict or competition. The crowns are identified in Scripture as the Incorruptible Crown (I Corinthians 9:25), the Crown of Rejoicing (I Thessalonians 2:19), the Crown of Righteousness (II Timothy 4:8), the crown of life (James

1:12), and the Crown of Glory (I Peter 5:4). Find these texts and read them for yourself. Then turn to Revelation 4:10-11 and see how we will take those crowns and cast them before the throne of God to magnify and glorify Him.

This experience will mark the beginning of our eternal life and service in God's presence. While everyone will be happy in heaven, there will surely be degrees of blessing, varying levels of glory, and different capacities for service. Consider I Corinthians 15:41-42a. *There is one glory of the sun, and another glory of the moon, and another glory of the stars: for one star differeth from another star in glory. So also is the resurrection.*

Can we understand all these things? No – to be sure. However, I know I don't want to waste my 60, 70, 80, 90 or so years here on earth investing in things that will not matter or count for the ages of the ages of the ages to come.

These challenges bring me back to our three original questions, which I pose to you again:

Who are you?

Why are you here?

Where are you going?

Husbands

Through my years of ministry experience, I have concluded that most men are not fully prepared to take on the challenge of becoming a husband, when they make their wedding vows. The commitments are for a lifetime, the pressures are unexpected, the responsibilities are great, and the uncertainties are many.

This brief article is not intended to prevent the challenges or solve all the problems that a husband might face, but it will focus on one issue that ultimately is the key to marital success. It comes out of one biblical text.

In Ephesians 5:25 the Apostle Paul wrote, *Husbands, love your wives, even as Christ loved the church, and gave himself for it...*

If a man understands this verse and commits himself to live it, he puts himself in a place where he can have the respect and trust of his wife, and the blessing and guidance of the Lord.

The first thing I encourage you to do is commit yourself to live out this verse the best you can. Is the husband of Ephesians 5:25, the man you want to be? If so, bow your head and declare it to God. It does not matter whether you are anticipating marriage, recently got married or have been married for many years. Make this declaration to God. You don't need to tell anyone else you have done it. Just determine that with God's help you are going to learn it and live it.

The challenge is easy to read – *Husbands, love your wives*. But, what is love? It is one of the most incredible terms you can find in Scripture. What helps us to understand it is the fact that there is more than one word from the original languages that can be translated love, in English. The term in Ephesians 5:25 is a term that is not related directly to emotion. When I tell my wife I love her, I am usually thinking of my feelings for her. But when I am told to love her as Christ loved the church, there is more to it than emotion. The term translated love, is *agape.* Underlying the meaning of *agape* is the concept of placing value on a person. Added to that, is the further idea of demonstrating the value I place on that person, by sacrificing for them. This is exactly what comes out of the challenge, when we are told to love our wives as *Christ loved the church and gave (sacrificed) himself for it.*

How do we put that kind of love into our marriage? It begins by understanding our God appointed role as a husband. We are each the leader of our family and the head of our wife. If we take that role in the strictest sense of its meaning, we have the right and responsibility to do what we want to do with our family, as long as we are not committing sin. It is understanding the role of being the head that actually opens the door for sacrifice. Some men abuse that role and thereby abuse their wife and family. As the head, I can control the money, the standards, the behavior, the activities and everything else in family life. Then God steps in and tells me I need to be willing to sacrifice my interests, so I can honor God in ministering to my family, in Christ like fashion. I am not a dictator, I am a leader who is to carry out his leadership responsibilities in accordance with God's instructions.

We need to step back and give thought to the broad implications of loving our wife, as Christ loved the church and gave himself for it. When Christ gave himself and sacrificed himself, it was not only His experience of dying on the cross; it was the results of His death mattered.

He was a Savior, not a martyr. When He died for us, He was making provision for everything we would ever need for time and eternity. He knew those needs and was sacrificing Himself to meet them. So, here I am as a husband, and I am told to love as Christ loved. To do that, there must be a willingness to sacrifice myself to meet my wife's needs. That, in turn, will require a conscientious effort to know her, understand her, and learn her needs. When I recognize those needs, I must make every effort to meet them, the best I can. That is loving, as Christ loved.

Let me suggest a few areas that demand our attention. A wife needs strong spiritual leadership. God made her the "helper"; He man the man the leader (Genesis 2:18). Does your wife see you as a man of God, a man of prayer, and a student of the scriptures? If not, there will be trouble in your home. Peter tells us women tend to be afraid to submit to their husband's leadership (I Peter 5:6). Do you intensify those fears by making foolish decisions or living a worldly life? A woman can be willful and will try to fix things when she sees they are not right Genesis 3:16; I Timothy 2:12–14). Has your wife tried to take control of your home and pressure you to do things her way? Maybe she is trying to fill the gap in leadership, because you have not stepped up to fulfill your God given obligations. Your wife needs physical, emotional and spiritual protection (Matthew 12:29), because she is vulnerable to attack in those areas.

Your wife is instructed by God to submit herself to the leadership of her husband. Some men try to throw that challenge at their wife, while announcing he is the head of the home. That guy never wins. Some men think that if they sacrifice their interests to minister to their wife's needs, they are submitting to her. Nothing could be further from the truth. If you are married, you are the head of your wife and the head of your home. It is not because you demand it or because she agrees. It is because God has appointed you to the task. It is true, you will need to earn your wife's trust and respect, because she tends to be willful and fearful. Take the challenge to be a man of God. Walk as a leader in your home, seeks God, studies His Word, and by grace, walks in spiritual wisdom. Pray for yourself. Pray for your wife. God wants your marriage to succeed.

You may be doing well right now or you may be struggling. Whatever your situation, ask God to help you be the man He wants you to be. Beware of the warning of Colossians 3:19, *Husbands, love your wives, and be not bitter against them.* God gives us such a warning, because bitterness is rooted in pride, and we men battle with pride. We are also given this warning, because our lady knows what button to push to anger, frustrate or embitter us. Love her. LOVE HER. **LOVE HER!**

LOVE HER, as Christ loved the church and gave himself for it.

Fathers

As with our comments on husbands, our thoughts about the role of a father will certainly not be exhaustive, but will focus on a few important truths.

Proverbs 17:6b says, *the glory of children are their fathers.* That is a powerful statement about the natural feelings of children toward their dads. Their dads are their glory. They love their dads, they hold them in high esteem; they boast about their dads and put them on a pedestal. Dads have a head-start in rearing and training their children, because they are held in high respect and honor. Unfortunately, too many dads fall off the pedestal

Fathers are instructed in Ephesians 6:4 to provoke not their children to wrath, but to bring them up in the nurture and admonition of the Lord. A similar challenge is found in Colossians 3:21, where fathers are told to provoke not their children *to anger*, lest they be discouraged. In each case there is the potential for very negative influence on a child. The child can become angry, bitter and discouraged by the words and actions of the very one that should be their pathway to Christ. When we find these kinds of specific challenges in scripture; it suggests that there is a tendency to fall in these areas. Evidently, fathers have a tendency to provoke their children. Instead, the father is told to bring children up in the nurture and admonition of the Lord. To nurture means to train, instruct, discipline, teach and chasten. All of this is to be done in a manner that magnifies and exalts the Lord. There is no place in a dad's life for yelling, harshness, or displays of temper. A quiet, strong testimony for Christ when correcting or directing a child will bring tremendous response from a young person. The other term for training used in Ephesians 6:4 is admonition. Admonition focuses more on words than action. We are to instruct our children in spiritual things in a spiritual way. The term means to put information into the mind of the child. Dads should teach their children how to live for Christ, how to handle problems and how to treat other people. Too few dads take on these obligations.

Some children grow up in anger and bitterness, because their dad was never there for them, or was angry and abusive in his ways. Some children will say they could never be good enough, smart enough or work hard enough to satisfy their dad. Dads need to be encouragers.

Every child is different. Some are compliant, some are stubborn, some are sneaky, some tend to lie and on it goes. The job of a dad is to understand the needs, struggles and problems of each of his children and minister to them in a way that wins them to himself and wins them to Christ.

One of the greatest obligations of a dad is to recognize that he is to portray to his child Godlike qualities, so the child will learn about God's character, by observing his dad's character. Facing that truth should sober any man. Psalm 103:13 illustrates the matter very well. The verse says, *Like as a father pitieth his children, so the LORD pitieth them that fear Him.* The term *pitieth* means to have understanding and compassion. Imagine trying to teach a child about the wonderful ways of God, and that He has understanding and compassion toward us, as His children. The text says, the LORD has understanding and compassion toward those that fear Him, just like a father has understanding and compassion toward his children. So a father says to his child, "The way

I treat you with understanding and compassion is how God will treat you." Wow! So what will they think about God? Will that bring our children to God or drive them away from God? Please do not take this lightly.

Another significant passage of Scripture is found in Paul's first letter to the Thessalonian believers. In verse 11 of chapter 2, Paul said, *As ye know how we exhorted you and comforted you and charged every one of you, as a father doth his children.* Paul said he did three things with these young believers, just like a father does with his children. First he *exhorted* them. That means he was their encourager to urge them toward spiritual grow and success. Secondly, he *comforted* them. The term comfort means soft speech. It is the whisper of consolation when someone does not perform successfully or up to expectation. Finally, he said he *charged* them. To charge means to summon as a witness. Be an encourager to your child and if he/she does not do well, comfort the child. If they did not do their best urge them on, but if they tried and failed seek to renew the spirit and confidence. The last challenge is extremely important. Charge them as a witness. Tell them they need to live like you do. They need to be diligent, loving, faithful, disciplined, kind, wise and gracious, just like you are. We need to consider what will happen if in fact our children act as we act. Will they be happy? Weill you be happy? Will God be happy?

Sometimes fathers leave child training to mom. No greater mistake could be made. Yes, a mother has an important role, but a dad is responsible for training his children in every area of life. He is a child's pathway to Christ. I have said and believe, when a child grows up in a Christian home and chooses the pathway of sin and worldliness, he has rejected his father, before he rejected the Lord. As a father, you are your child's glory; don't fail that precious gift from God.

Stepfathers
Counting the Cost of Success

Introductory thoughts

I am sure my adolescent years were not unique, but they were certainly interesting. My folks were divorced when I was about three years of age. I never really knew my father and for years did not care to, since he showed no interest in the family. When my mother announced she was remarrying, I was excited about it. I was about 13 years old and felt very happy that I was going to have a dad. My mother had four children, though when she married my stepfather, only two of us were still at home. My stepfather also had four children and two of his were still at home. When the marriage took place in June of 1958, a few things became evident immediately. My mother's spirit of independence, my stepfather's drinking problem, and ensuing conflict over the children were going to make for a very rocky road. From my perspective, disagreement over the children was the number one difficulty. In fact, the newly "blended" family did not make it past Christmas under the same roof. In less than six months the marriage fell on hard times. It was not until late in my senior year of high school that my mother and stepfather tried to live together again. That second attempt lasted less than one year. Only once all the children were grown up and out of the house, did they have an acceptable relationship together.

During those years we were religious, but lost. If we had known the Lord Jesus it could have made a difference, but all would agree, that being saved in itself does not guarantee a happy home for the natural family or the stepfamily. For every family, careful obedience and submission to the Scriptural teaching on family life is the only hope. That very fact suggests that stepfamilies will have a hard time, because most of them, as with my own family, are born out of the tragedy of divorce and its accompanying rejection of God's Word. With a shaky foundation, it is hard to build a solid structure. However, even if the stepfamily originates from a situation where a mate has been widowed, there are pressures that make unity and harmony difficult to attain. The stepfamily must go the second mile in adherence to the Scriptures in order to have the goodness of God's blessings. I hope my growing up experience coupled with truth from God's Word will provide encouragement for any who face the challenge of the stepfamily.

This appendix is written to offer hope and insights for the stepfather, to help him have the best possible chance for success, in a situation where some would say, there are already two strikes against him. Dad is the God appointed leader of the family. His walk with Christ and spiritual wisdom will, to a great degree, determine the happiness and stability of the home. With this being true in the natural family, it is of utmost importance in the stepfamily.

The challenge

Being a dad in a stepfamily is one of the greatest family challenges of our day. It is estimated that one in every four children growing up during the 1990's and beyond, in the United States, will eventually be in a stepfamily setting. Over 90% of those children will live with their biological mother and a stepfather. So, if you are a stepfather, you are not alone. Consider with me some information, from a variety of sources concerning stepfamilies, to help define the challenge associated with this quickly growing position in the American home. For instance, the stepfamily faces pressures that are unique. One or both mates may have a former spouse, former in-laws, and children from a previous marriage. Most partners in these marital settings admit they had little comprehension how tough it would be to combine two families. They are apparently unprepared for the fact that the stepfamily is an unnatural social setting which will not readily yield to developing relationships with the same ease as in the natural family. In simple terms, it is a whole lot easier to develop love and patience for your biological child than for the child of another. Add to that the fact that the stepfamily is often created following the heartache and bitterness that accompanies divorce. When all the elements are factored in, it is no surprise that serious problems often arise as couples establish stepfamily relationships and children try to respond to their new situation. It is no wonder that the second marriage often yields to these pressures and consequently fails at a much higher rate than first marriages. Take heed, to be successful as a stepfather, is no easy task.

Facing the facts

Many times a single mother seeks to remarry, believing a father for her children is vitally necessary for their physical and emotional welfare. Such marriages however, do not reproduce a normal family structure. Children in stepfamilies are found to have as many or more behavioral problems than those living in single-parent homes. Up to 75% of stepchildren repeat a grade in school and those same children are 70% more likely to be expelled, than children living with their natural parents. Surveys show that stepchildren struggle with loneliness and run away in disproportionately large numbers. It is evident they have great difficulty adjusting to their new family setting. To conquer these problems will require uncommon devotion from a step dad to his children.

No doubt most men take on the role of stepfather with high hopes of success and a strong desire to meet the needs of new family members, however the stepfather will seldom, if ever, "replace" a child's natural father. No matter how irresponsible a biological father may have been toward his children, they will generally hold him in high esteem. As a stepfather struggles with developing the necessary balance of love and control toward his children and wrestles to define his role in guidance, care and discipline, he can experience much frustration. Perhaps this frustration is part of the reason why children in stepfamilies are more likely to experience harsh parental discipline than their peers in the natural family setting. Obviously such cases are not acceptable.

A wise stepfather will also realize that children are often caught in the middle of parental conflicts, fearing that love to a stepfather may be perceived as disloyalty to a biological father. Sadly, adults often foster those fears by negative words and actions.

Needless to say, this information is not very encouraging. Thank the Lord, your family can be different, but to be successful as a stepfather one must face some hard realities and respond to them with spiritual grace and insight.

Guidelines to help

Whether we like it or not, the role of the stepfather will vary from family to family dependent on acceptance by the children, the involvement of the children's natural father and other factors that are beyond his control. The Apostle Paul learned to be content in whatsoever state he found himself (Phil. 4:11). He expressed his confidence for success with these words; "I can do all things through Christ which strengtheneth me" (Phil. 4:13). A stepfather must find contentment with his circumstances and determine by faith to do all things through Christ as the source of his strength.

The first priority in facing any spiritual challenge is one's personal walk with the Lord. Every family will face many pressures which will require spiritual wisdom to endure. A stepfather must provide true spiritual leadership. Church involvement, prayer, devotional time and a spiritual response to difficult situations are essential. If you succumb to spiritual defeat and discouragement, the family will fall when you fall. Your family must be able to see Christ in you. As Colossians 2:6,7 says, "As ye have received Christ Jesus the Lord, so walk ye in him: rooted and built up in him, and stablished in the faith, as ye have been taught, abounding therein with thanksgiving." In simple terms, you need to be a growing Christian. Pressures either drive us to the Lord or drive us away from Him. You need to make sure they drive you to Him. To handle difficult situations in the wisdom of the flesh will usually make things worse than when they started. When searching the Scriptures and praying we can come up with the answers we need for the challenge at hand. It is not enough, however, to simply open the Bible during a crisis and hope the solution will jump off the page at us. Spiritual wisdom comes through consistent and continual study of the Word of God. Gradually, wisdom is developed and the principles of Scripture are built into our lives. There are no short cuts to maturity. Start today, there will be rich dividends in the days ahead.

The second priority in life for a married man, is to strengthen his marriage. Marriages established with the best of circumstances are shaken by the storms of life. A stepfather must commit himself to being the best husband he can be. Your marriage may be a second try for you or your wife, or maybe both. If so, there has been a tremendous amount of spiritual and emotional baggage brought into your relationship that may take a heavy toll on you. You will need to go the second mile in communication, tenderness and understanding. You will have to fight off selfishness, and its companion self-pity, especially when you feel like you are giving and giving in your marriage, but never seem to get much in return. The challenge, to love your wife as Christ loved the church, is one that you must heed daily. That love is best understood as the sacrifice of one's self for another. That is your primary marital responsibility. You will have to work hard to develop and keep a close relationship with your wife. Usually when a young couple gets married, they have a couple of years without children. This gives them time to get to know each other more fully and work through the needed adjustments to get the marriage on a good foundation. As a stepfather you were not afforded that benefit. Consequently, the earliest months of your marriage included one or more children to fit into the adjustment period. Whatever the particulars of your situation may be, you will need a love that can only be produced by the Spirit of God, in order to give and give and give again. Remember though, there are no other options.

Though it may be difficult, recognize that you are probably not going to "replace" the natural father of your stepchildren, especially if there has been a divorce and he is still living. Proverbs 17:6b says, "... the glory of children are their fathers". God has secured in the hearts of children, a special place for their dad. Experience demonstrates that children often maintain a loyalty to their natural father in spite of the fact that he may have failed, abused or hurt them. For two years, during my college days, my wife and I were house parents in a Children's Home. We basically had the children with us as if they were our own. On one weekend a month they were scheduled to be with their parents, or parent, as the case might be. Many of these children could have been home, but they were not wanted. One set of three, two brothers and a sister, were caught in the divorce tragedy. Their parents divorced and each remarried. In the new marriage setting, neither wanted the children from their first marriage, so the kids ended up in the Home. There were other situations equally bizarre. The amazing fact was, that all the children maintained incredible loyalty to their natural parents.

To a large degree then, your role in the lives of your stepchildren will depend on their willingness to accept you. You may feed them, clothe them, and meet many of their needs without ever receiving the love and appreciation you may want or expect. You must handle this spiritually and not fall into the trap of hurt, anger or bitterness. You may be tempted to remind the children of their father's failures, but to do so will only bring hurt to the very ones you want to help. Let their father's deeds, good or bad, speak for themselves. Accept your role with grace, work hard to earn their respect, and seek to have great spiritual impact on their lives.

You must make every attempt to be involved in the lives and activities of your stepchildren. It is hard when your efforts may not seem to be appreciated, but you need to work to be respected and accepted. The children did not ask for their situation; they have had their choices made for them. That stepchildren tend to feel lonely and too often run away, is a signal that some very important aspects of stepfamily relationships are generally ignored or handled poorly. A single mom often pours her life into her children. She tries to make up for the absence of their dad and sometimes gains emotional support for herself by involvement with them. The stepfather enters the family, but instead of filling the void left by the absent father, he is often perceived by the children as taking mom away. It is true that marriage is the primary family relationship and yours will require much time and effort. At the same time, your stepchildren must see you as a loving and devoted addition to their family, not someone who is robbing them of their only source of security and stability, namely, their mother. You must be a very real and supportive presence in their day to day lives and acknowledge that when you married their mother you accepted them as a permanent part of your future.

One of the most dividing problems in the stepfamily is the discipline and training of the children. This whole realm will demand a great deal of communication and agreement between you and your spouse. The natural parent has both the right and responsibility to address these areas, but your role must be carefully established and defined. Your goal is to achieve as natural a setting as possible, because you are the head of the home. A major question is, does your wife have enough confidence in you, to allow you a free hand in the care of "her" children? If she does, how will the children respond? Many stepfathers have fared well with the children until a crisis in a disciplinary situation. The words, "you have no right . . . you are not my real father", have pierced many stepdads' hearts. A very positive response of love, firmness and encouragement will provide the best chance to establish a strong and lasting bond. The needed message to the child is the same that a biological father might give, "I love you, but you must obey". For a stepfather, the difficulty of success is multiplied a dozen times, but success is a must. The children may seek to drive a wedge between you and your spouse. If they succeed, the whole family will face years of heartache and turmoil. Solid agreement on standards, curfews, chore responsibilities and disciplinary procedures will put stepfamilies far ahead of many natural families, in maintaining good order in the home. When discipline is necessary, it must be carried out in a God honoring fashion. Remember, discipline is not merely punishment for disobedience; it is correctional, with a view toward the future. It is an opportunity to teach valuable lessons and strengthen the bond between parent and child. Never let the time of discipline be reflective of the frustration you might feel toward the whole stepfamily experience.

For every child, emotional security stands out as a very important need. As a stepfather, you must seek to meet that need and be sure your presence and actions do not undermine your child's welfare. As has already been suggested, you dare not be viewed as taking the children's mother away from them, but instead, must devote yourself to being a participant in the children's lives. It is not unusual for a stepchild to threaten to run away, believing he can find a home with his "real" father or his paternal grandparents. At such times the child needs assurance of love and a statement affirming that he is wanted, already has a home, and is staying right where he is. Too often the frustrated stepfather offers to help pack the suitcase or buy the plane ticket for the move. This kind of response convinces the child that his thinking was correct, his stepfather does not really care. Along the same line and perhaps even worse, is the threat to send a child to live with someone else, if he does not shape up. These warnings are the most destructive comments that can be made to stepchildren. They convey that love is conditional and that the parent-child relationship will continue only as long as it is convenient and not too much trouble. The toughest child on the outside is too fragile on the inside to bear the hurt that accompanies such remarks.

As a stepfather, you have a unique opportunity to play a special role in the life of one or more children. There is little hope that it will be an easy task and, in fact, may be characterized by unrequited love and unappreciated effort. If you will pay the price of sacrificial love, and fulfill your role with eternity's values in view, you may be granted the blessed privilege of salvaging, from the heartache of this world, the greatest commodity on earth, a child. Surely, He who is the father of the fatherless (Psalm 68:5), will grant you mercy, strength and help.

Covering all of the bases

Not all the subject matter in this last section will be received well by some, but we deal with it in the spirit of Proverbs 27:6, "Faithful are the wounds of a friend". The intent of these words is to help stepfathers have the best possible opportunity to be successful in a family setting fraught with difficulties. To accomplish that goal, it is necessary for these added words of caution and encouragement.

There are multiplied sources of help for families, including books, video tapes, counselors, etc., but let all remember our hope is in the Lord. The Scriptures inform us that sometimes we shut ourselves off from His help by various kinds of sin and iniquity. This warning will not apply to all, but it may be appropriate for you. Often the stepfamily exists because God's Word has been ignored or intentionally violated, resulting in the dissolution of a first marriage. Sins of the past can haunt a relationship and hinder the blessing of God. If you are reading this booklet in anticipation of an upcoming marriage that will make you a stepfather, consider these thoughts. If there has been divorce in your past, or that of the one you plan to marry, and either of your previous mates are still living, you will be committing adultery if you get married (Mark 10: 11,12). Such a marriage is not in the will of God for you. (For further guidance see our booklet, "Marriage, Divorce, and Remarriage"). If you are already a stepfather and your current marriage occurred after you or your wife had been divorced, be sure you have faced your past honestly before the Lord. The Apostle John teaches us in 1 John 1:9, that if we confess our sins, God is faithful and just to forgive our sins and to cleanse us from all unrighteousness. The past cannot be changed, but hope for the future is found in the assurance of sweet fellowship with the Lord. If there is sin from your past that needs to be confessed, deal with it today. Be sure nothing is in your life that might hinder God from giving the fullness of his blessing to you and your family. To give your family the best chance for happiness, get right in every way with the Lord and with people. Seek forgiveness from anyone you may have hurt and, equally as important, forgive any and all who may have hurt you.

Parental agreement in rearing one's natural children is not easy to attain for a husband and wife. To achieve it consistently and effectively in the stepfamily can be much tougher. As a stepfather you must be spiritually and emotionally prepared for this challenge. The burden will be even greater if you have children from a previous marriage that live with you, or if you and your present wife have children together. As the husband and father in your family, you should set the standards of discipline and practice in your home. You must establish the spiritual direction of your home and keep everyone moving in that direction. To do these tasks well, you must guard against any form of favoritism in your own actions, and protect your children from favoritism shown by others. Love, support, kindness and firmness must be equally meted out to all. Material benefits as mundane as food, toys, clothing and education must be equally available. You must strive for a balance that often eludes the average natural family. To accomplish this, you may battle your own feelings or you may have to slow down a well- meaning relative who wants to make up for the seeming deprivation suffered by one of the children. As with other of your obligations, this can be a tough one to carry out, and in some instances be almost impossible, because of grandparents and other relatives. It will not be an easy task and, unfortunately, one more of those challenges that seldom come to the natural family, but often faces the stepfamily.

An area more delicate than all the rest must also be addressed. As unpleasant as it is to consider, statistics reveal that molestation and sexual abuse occur in unusually high percentages in the stepfamily. Proverbs 9:9 says, "Give instruction to a wise man, and he will be yet wiser . . ." In the spirit of that verse I share these concerns. Sometimes problems occur among the stepchildren. A typical case might involve an older stepbrother taking advantage of a younger stepsister. The two children are not biologically related and yet find themselves in circumstances generally reserved for the natural family. Common practices of indiscretion that would mean nothing to natural siblings can lead to trouble among step siblings. These could include how young people might dress in the relaxed setting of home or that they might often be left alone when parents are working or out socially. The wise parent will be alert to these dangers without being unfairly judgmental toward their children. More often, however, abuse is found when a stepfather misuses a stepdaughter. The situation is the same as with the siblings. In our homes, we tend to be less discreet in our actions than we would ever be in public. Unfortunately, lusts that would virtually never arise in a man toward his biological daughter, may be stirred up toward a stepdaughter. Some will be offended at these warnings, but no one is exempt from sin. It is the product of the flesh (Galatians 5:18-21), and we all are still plagued with the sinful nature. Victory over sin comes by walking in the Spirit (Galatians 5:22-23), guarding our eyes (Psalm 101:2-3) and fleeing temptation (1 Corinthians 6:18). Your personal standards of purity, prudence and discretion must be kept very high. Heeding Paul's warning in Romans 13:14 has preserved many from getting into situations where sin might occur. He said, "But put ye on the Lord Jesus Christ, and make not provision for the flesh, to fulfill the lusts thereof." To not make provision for the flesh means to avoid those situations where there is even the slightest possibility that Satan could get us to fall. You may be one of the few stepfathers who can earn the full trust and respect of his stepchildren. Do not violate that trust, because it is very rare and precious. Beg God to establish and preserve in your home, a wholesome atmosphere of peace, happiness and virtue.

Concluding thoughts

It would seem logical that first marriages and natural families have a far better chance for success than second marriages and stepfamilies. When one enters a stepfamily relationship there is usually emotional and spiritual baggage that comes along. All the pressures that come to bear on the natural family are increased and all the obstacles to success are enlarged. Many fail to see the full picture and do not count the cost involved in making the stepfamily successful. The fact is that the divorced person should remain single, or as Paul said in 1 Corinthians 7:11, be reconciled to one's original mate. If you are divorced or contemplating marrying a divorced person, I would exhort you to remain single. God's desire is that the bond of marriage never be broken, but by death (Matthew 19:4-5). He wants one man to stay with one woman for life.

If you are in a second marriage, there will be much to overcome to achieve the measure of happiness you desire. The demand for love, patience, communication, understanding and self-sacrifice, commonly required in a first marriage, will be multiplied for you. It will take work and creativity to conquer the pitfalls generally encountered in the stepfamily.

Thankfully, our God is the God of all grace (1 Peter 5:10) and his grace is sufficient to meet our every need (II Corinthians 12:9). Determine to be the man you must be to make your family live in peace, harmony and the joy of the Lord. Then make it happen, one day at a time. Count the cost and be willing to pay the price of success. Second marriages end in divorce at an amazing rate of 65%. Your marriage can be part of the 35% that make it and of the far lower percentage of people that genuinely have a good marriage. Children of divorced parents are far more likely to get divorced than children who grow up with both biological parents. By God's grace and through careful adherence to the teachings of scripture, your children can be different. What price must be paid for success? The price will be unusual dedication to following all the Bible says about family life and unusual personal surrender to the Savior's lordship. Dad, to a great degree, you will determine the success of your family. Face the challenge realistically and face the challenge spiritually.

Grandfathers

Proverbs 17:6a says, *Children's children are the crown of old men.* A crown is a symbol of victory and joy. A grandchild is a special treasure and brings incredible joy to a grandfather. A grandfather must provide a godly example to his grandchildren and be able to give godly counsel, when it is sought.

Our desire should be to give our grandchildren a strong testimony for Christ. In Psalm 71:18, the Psalmist wrote, *Now also when I am old and gray headed, O God, forsake me not; until I have shewed thy strength unto this generation, and thy power to everyone that is to come.* I interpret the words of the Psalmist as his desire to not die until he could show his family the greatness of God. That is the role of the grandfather. The testimony of David in Psalm 37:23-25 is wonderful. He said, *The steps of a good man are ordered by the LORD and he delighteth in his way. Though he fall, he shall not be utterly cast down: for the LORD upholdeth him with his hand. I have been young and now am old; yet have I not seen the righteous forsaken, nor his seed begging bread.* These are powerful words that can best be spoken by a grandfather. David was speaking as an old man who had watched the hand of God for a life time – his own life and others. He tells young people that their steps can be guided by the LORD, if they will serve Him. Even if they stumble along the way, the LORD will hold them up and He will never forsake them. Our grandchildren need to hear from us that it is worth it to serve God for a lifetime. May Christ be seen in us.

There some ways in which a grandfather must be cautious. Every grandfather has seen his children handle their children differently than Grandpa would. Sometimes they are too strict; sometimes they are too permissive. The wise grandfather will say more to the Lord about the situation than he will to his children. We sometimes want to intervene, but we must remember God gave our grandchildren to our children, not to us. Pray for your children and your grandchildren every day. I like to think of being available for counsel and advice, rather than being too pushy. When a son or daughter asks for parenting advice, we have a chance to be a positive influence.

We need to be careful to not get in between our children and our grandchildren. It is not unusual for grandparents to undermine their children's authority. Grandchildren in a strict family may be told, "I know you can't do that at your house, but when you are with us it is okay." Grandchildren in a permissive family might be told, "You might get away with that with your parents, but you are not going to act that way here." You might feel the need to do things differently with your grandchildren when they are in your home. If so, do it, but don't compare your children unfavorably with yourself.

Be careful of favoritism. For whatever reason grandparents often have a favorite grandchild. It may be the first grandchild. It may be the little girl whose sibling are all boys. It may be the child who has physical traits that favor the family. It may be the quiet compliant child rather than the little rascal. In any event. IT IS UNACCEPTABLE! Isaac favored Esau and Rebecca favored Jacob. The family was a disaster. Then Jacob was foolish enough to favor Joseph. It produced another generation of heartache.

I have been blessed to have some of my grandchildren call me for advice. My first question has always been. What do your parents say? Make sure you lift up their parents in their eyes. If there is an extreme situation of harshness or abuse from your grandchild's parent to your grandchild, be very careful how you respond. Pray. Beg God for wisdom. Make sure you have as much information as possible, before you enter into that matter.

One of the most important things you can provide for your grandchildren is what I will call generational emotional and spiritual security. You may not always have the opportunity to say things you might want to say, but just your life of solid testimony for Christ, will be a powerful witness to your grandchildren. They may stray in actions or even in belief, but if they can look to you and see Christ in your life, it will provide an immovable wall of protection. When they want help, they will know where to turn. Never write them off, even if they break your heart.

Appendix E

HOW TO BE SURE YOU ARE GOING TO HEAVEN

There is one God who created the world. All of us, who live in the world, are doomed to die, but we are not like animals. When an animal dies its existence is over. When a man dies it only affects his body, because every man has an immortal soul. When he dies the soul leaves the body and continues to exist. The question is, what will happen to you after you die? The Bible says there are two eternal destinations. The one is hell; the other is heaven. Tragically, the Bible says most people will go to hell.

The issue is simple. God is holy, but men are sinners, and to enter heaven they must be cleansed of their sin. How can that be accomplished?

Begin by recognizing yourself as a sinner. Very few people would deny that fact. Now, forget about religion. If you are faithful in attending a church or if you never darken the church door – forget it. See yourself as a sinful man standing before a holy God. God loves you and has done something to deal with your sin, if you will receive it. John 3:16 is a well-known Bible verse. Consider it. *For God so loved the world, that he gave his only begotten son, that whosoever believeth in him, should not perish, but have everlasting life.*

There is the message of salvation. God's only begotten son is Jesus Christ. As you may know, Jesus came to this earth to die on the cross of Calvary to cleanse us of our sin. In order to not perish in hell, but have everlasting life in heaven, we need to believe in him. Belief is not just mental assent to the facts of his death. Belief is faith. It means to put your weight on something, so you are depending on it to hold you. We get saved by putting all our hope on Jesus Christ, believing that faith in him will save us and cleanse us.

Being sure of heaven does not come through religion. It does not come through baptism, communion, church attendance or trying to live a good life. To believe in Christ means rejecting everything else and trusting in Jesus Christ alone. The Bible says God put our sins on Christ when Christ shed his blood and died on the cross for us.

Read these verses:

Isaiah 53:6: *All we like sheep have gone astray; we have turned everyone to his own way; and the LORD hath laid on him the iniquity of us all.*

II Corinthians 5:21: *For he hath made him to be sin for us, who knew no sin; that we might be made the righteousness of God in him.*

Romans 5:8: *But God commendeth his love toward us, in that, while we were yet sinners, Christ died for us.*

I Peter 5:24: *Who his own self bare our sins in his own body on the tree, that we being dead to sins, should live unto righteousness: by whose stripes we are healed.*

Can you see it? God put our sin on Christ. Romans 10:13 says, *Whosoever shall call upon the name of the Lord shall be saved?* If you want your sin forgiven and you want to be sure of heaven, get down on your knees or bow your head and ask the God of heaven to save you. Tell him you are putting your faith in Jesus Christ and nothing else, because accept Christ's death on the cross as payment for your sin. Do it now. God will not reject your tender heart.

If you have done it, you have this promise from I John 5:13. *These things have I written unto you that believe on the name of the son of God; that ye may know that ye have eternal life, and that ye may believe on the name of the son of God.*

If you have put your faith in Jesus Christ for salvation, find a good Bible believing church and begin to worship there. Get baptized as a testimony of your faith in Christ. Tell others that you have trusted Christ.

If we can help, contact us.

Write to Biblical Family Ministries, P.O. Box 285, Myerstown, PA 17067 or email to eagbfm@comcast.net (E. Allen Griffith)

About the Author

E. Allen Griffith is the Executive Director of Biblical Family Ministries Inc., which he founded in 1993. Previously he served as pastor of the Bible Baptist Church of West Chester, Pennsylvania for 26 years. Dr. Griffith has produced a variety of books and CDs on the family, Christian life and other topics. He speaks regularly at Family Life Conferences and carries on a counseling ministry. He and his wife Patricia live in Lebanon, PA. They have 5 children, 18 grandchildren and a growing number of great grandchildren.

CPSIA information can be obtained
at www.ICGtesting.com
Printed in the USA
BVHW080140140519
548199BV00006B/13/P